# PADDLIN'
## with
# THOREAU

### Reflections from the RED Kayak

## By Mary Anne Smrz

*Paddlin' with Thoreau: Reflections from the Red Kayak*

Published in the United States by Mary Anne Smrz

Cover Design by Ann Moss
Front Cover photo by Dee Beckmann
Back Cover photo of Mary Anne by Andrea Kells

All photographs by Mary Anne Smrz unless otherwise noted

Printed in the United States

ISBN-13: 978-1-7325578-7-1

The purpose of this book is to inspire and comfort. The information is designed to acquaint individuals with the process of journaling as a way to gain insight. Neither the author nor the publisher is engaged in rendering medical or counseling advice. If such advice is required, the services of a qualified medical professional should be sought. The author and publisher shall not be held liable or responsible to any person or entity with respect to any loss or damage caused or alleged to be caused, directly or indirectly by the information contained in this publication.

1-Thoreau 2-Journaling 3-Spirituality 4-Nature
5-Kayaking 6-Self-Help 7-Water

Email:          info@redkayak.net
Website:      www.redkayak.net

## Dedication

| To my Mom, | | my Great-Niece, |
| Toni Smrz, | and | Bianca Murawski, |
| Age 93 | | Age 1 |

*You are a beautiful enduring arc
across the generations of our family,
one end graced with timeless wisdom
and the other blessed with
hope and promise for the future.*

The *Reflections from the Red Kayak* series surfaced from over 27 years of tranquil paddling excursions. An insightful inner journey to find authenticity and wholeness, the trilogy encourages others to embark on the same. Thought provoking questions at the end of each essay allow readers to journal their own thoughts and reflections.

*All three books from the*
*Reflections from the Red Kayak trilogy are*
*available on Amazon.com.*

**Reflections from the Red Kayak: Thoughts on Life**

**A Season on the Water: Reflections from the Red Kayak**

**Change: Our Ever-Present Companion:**
**Reflections from the Red Kayak**

For more information or to sign up for our inconsistent and irregular newsletter, please visit our website at www.redkayak.net.

Thank you and keep paddlin' on...

*"Could a greater miracle take place than for us to look through each other's eyes for an instant?"*

Henry David Thoreau
*Walden,* Economy

Trust the truth
of your journey.
Live simply with nature.
Keep paddlin' on...

May Ar

# Table of Contents

vii

# Table of Contents (cont'd)

# Table of Contents (cont'd)

# Table of Contents (cont'd)

# Prologue

*"Books must be read as deliberately and reservedly as they were written. Books are the treasured wealth of the world and the fit inheritance of generations and nations."*

*– Henry David Thoreau, Walden, Reading*

There is someone I'd like you to meet. For many years, I have been on a journey with him, pulled in by the power of his connection to nature. Although he is not physically here, the distant voice of his wisdom reverberates through his writings today.

As my virtual traveling companion, his philosophy on life and nature guides me like a beacon of light. He is a good friend of mine. Like all good friends, we come to know each other better by spending quality time together. Several years ago, I decided to do just that.

It all began in November, 2019. I met him at the most poignant place, Walden Pond, where he took my hand and said, "Walk with me." For the next few years, I stepped deeper into his life, immersing myself in his books and books written about him. Together he and I hiked his paths, paddled his waters and summited his mountains.

His name is Henry. Henry David Thoreau. I call him HDT for short. All good friends have nicknames.

He was born over 200 years ago on July 12, 1817, in Concord, Massachusetts. The insights and wisdom in his writings during his short life continue to amaze me. Reading his challenging text in early 19th century prose is often difficult to decipher, but as a wise sage, his profound messages are clear.

Henry was deeply influenced by his friend, Ralph Waldo Emerson. Emerson's essay, "Nature," which emphasizes the importance of nature as an expression of the divine spirit, imprinted itself onto Thoreau. As a result of their friendship, Thoreau became a leading figure in transcendentalism, part of the "liveliest intellectual movement of nineteenth-century America."[1]

"The Transcendentalist movement held, as one of its premises, that the human connection with nature is necessary for intellectual and moral stability."[2] Thoreau believed in living a life with meaning and found his answers in the sanctuary of the natural world.

My friendship with Henry grew. Every day, prior to writing, I conversed with him. I looked at his picture on the cover of *Meditations of Henry David Thoreau: A Light in the Woods*, which sat perched on my Thoreau desk. Through his eyes, I clearly saw the path of simplicity.

This ritual led to my selection of his opening quote, *"Could a greater miracle take place than for us to look through each other's eyes for an instant?"*[3] I looked through Henry's eyes to channel his wisdom forward. Our virtual friendship continued to blossom as I bridged his thoughts from yesterday with my insights for today.

To build the bridge, I modeled this quote about Henry which was noted in the introduction of his journal, "...he continued to integrate facts of nature with facts of the spirit."[4]

For my essays, I linked a selected Thoreau quote to his circumstances while writing it and facts of nature. To enhance the bridge, I added a photo or pencil sketch pertaining to my essay. I included pencil sketches to honor J. Thoreau & Co. Pencils, his family-owned pencil factory, one of the finest of that time.

I then integrated my insights with facts of the spirit. These essays on the span of the bridge conclude with questions for you to ponder. A blank page or two for your own musings or pencil sketches completes the structure. I added a small pencil sketch of Thoreau's desk at the bottom of the pages so you, too, can write on "his desk."

The essays are meant to be read slowly, allowing their meaning to blend with your thoughts and feelings. The book is filled with connections – bridges, arcs, rainbows, curves, turns, bends – reminding us of the unifying continuity that keeps us in relationship to all of life. We paddle on the same continuous stream. We all stay afloat or sink together.

Books ride an unending arc on an infinite continuum, a perpetual bridge connecting past and present, guiding us to the future. They keep the author's wisdom alive, communicating from a long ago point of significance.

Henry's messages are more important today than ever. I feel that we often look in the wrong places for our answers. Problems cannot be solved with the same mindset that created them. Nature teaches us how to live with authenticity, providing a refreshing alternative for the answers we desperately need. There is no better truth than nature.

Henry and I share an insightful journey down a well-worn trail, filled with timeless nuggets of nature's lessons. Once on his path, everything becomes a lesson in truth and simplicity.

My friendship with HDT unfolds on these pages. I invite you to meet him and let him take you by the hand to embrace his universal truths and perpetual wisdom.

We will saunter on his paths, where he was grounded in his own truths. We will paddle his waters, where his congruent flow preserved his own true course. And we will summit his mountains as he elevated himself to a higher purpose.

It is my hope that you will receive the words and messages longing to surface from within, bringing deeper meaning, an enduring love of nature and the clarity of truth and simplicity to your life.

Let my friend, Henry lead the way across the bridge.

Keep paddlin' on....

Mary Anne Smrz, April 11, 2023

My Thoreau Library

# Stars on the Water and in the Heavens

*"The water shines with an inward light
like a heaven on earth."*

-Henry David Thoreau, Journal, June 13, 1851, Age 33

At the age of 20, Thoreau took his first solo sea voyage to Maine. He quit his short-lived teaching job in Concord because he did not agree with the use of corporal punishment to discipline his students, and went in search of meaningful work.

He borrowed $10 from Ralph Waldo Emerson for the journey and left on May 3, 1838. He sailed from Boston to Castine, Maine, arriving on May 13th. After four days in Maine, he sailed back.

He did not find an educator teaching opportunity on this voyage, but after a short while, he and his brother, John, opened a private school in Concord, Massachusetts. He also began his involvement with the family pencil business, establishing J. Thoreau & Co. Pencils as one of the highest quality of the time.

Pencil sketch from photo of plankton "stars" on the water

## The Awe of Insignificance
### September 30, 2021

*I purposely begin this book with Henry's story of his first seafaring voyage to Castine, Maine, having had the incredible opportunity to kayak off the shores of Castine. At the time, I did not know of the connection to Henry on these same waters in Penobscot Bay. Once realized, it seemed the perfect start for* Paddlin' with Thoreau...

*There are a handful places in the world, such as Costa Rica, Puerto Rico, Florida and a few others, where the unforgettable experience of a bioluminescent kayak excursion is possible. Castine's Harbor is one of these magical places, creating the perfect environment for these underwater "fireflies."*

*What is a bioluminescent paddling experience, you ask?*

*A wonder-filled nighttime adventure paddling in an area of an abundance of glowing plankton, who live and thrive in unique ecosystems.*

*This much anticipated trip begins with Castine Kayak Adventures, a local outfitter, leading us on our shimmering water journey this September evening.*

*The setting is idyllic, beginning with the arc of a colorful rainbow over the harbor after a quick evening rainstorm. Just enough rain to get our kayak seats wet! Water, water, everywhere. Yet the rainbow is our first of many gifts.*

*Our guide takes us out as the misty gray camouflage of dusk settles in, offering us an opportunity to feel the foreign sensation being on the water as darkness envelopes us. Leaving the comfort of the harbor lights, we venture out in our tandem kayaks beyond a few islands into the approaching blackness of nightfall.*

Far from shore, we enter obscure areas, and are greeted by a brilliant lightshow on the water. With every stroke of our paddles, a trail of luminescent plankton follow, like sparklers on the water. The lights of the plankton emit a flashing glow when disturbed by motion. It is dazzling! I never experienced the bliss of being surrounded by "shooting stars" on the water. The farther out we paddle, the darker the water, the brighter the plankton's radiance.

How many times in our lives, when things seem the darkest, do we dip our paddle into that blackness and find some shimmer of light? From the darkest dark, the brightest of light shines in contrast. They flow together, dark and light, and remind us we need both for balance to live a rich and meaningful life.

As the night progresses, the clouds from the earlier storm dissipate, and a blizzard of pulsating stars emerges through the blackness of the celestial heavens, the Milky Way a creamy silk arch streaming across the sky. It, too, was dazzling – the stars overhead complementing the stars on the water. I feel serene being suspended between heaven and earth, one of those times when the rest of life is irrelevant. The opaqueness of the night adds to the suspended feeling of hovering somewhere "out there." The horizon is indistinguishable and only our limited senses ground us to the experience, rendering us speechless.

Our group rafts up together and our guide points out the visible constellations. His precise descriptions provide the guidance to easily identify the patterns of the zodiac. "The everlasting geometry of the stars,"[1] as Henry wrote, is our astrological wonder.

We sit silently in that space for what seems like an eternity, gazing upward, mesmerized by both the millions of points of light in the sky and looking downward at the swirling shimmers of light on the water. It was an experience of complete surrender to something larger, something grander, something beyond comprehension.

7

There are times in my life when I feel insignificant, sometimes not in the best way. Life's experiences and people can negatively impact me, creating a sense of irrelevance. But tonight the feeling of insignificance is peaceful and calming, as though someone else or something larger than me is in control. I am a tiny speck in the eye of the universe.

In close watch of the sky, we witness brilliant shooting stars treating us to the startling wonder of the infinite cosmos. In his journal, Henry wrote "We look upward for inspiration."[2] This night, surrounded by glowing lights swirling as if in an illuminated snow globe, inspiration abounds.

We kayak back to shore, the dim harbor lights in the distance our guide, the plankton by our side, shooting out "stars of light" on the water. Safely back on land, the feeling of peaceful insignificance remains. I write this story but truthfully, there are no words to adequately describe the eternal feeling of awe and connection this night.

*************

Can you name a time in your life when you were deeply in awe or wonder of an experience?

Do you remember the feeling it gave you?

How does insignificance feel to you? Was there a time when it felt peaceful or felt awful? What was the difference in the experience that created those feelings?

# Thoreau

9

10

# A Week on the Concord and Merrimack Rivers
## Published May 30, 1848, Age 30

*A Week* is the first of Thoreau's two books published during his lifetime. It is the moving story of an introspective river journey with his older brother, John, in 1839, when Thoreau was 22 years old.

From their home in Concord, Massachusetts, they boated on the Concord River to the Merrimack River and into New Hampshire. They hiked the White Mountains then returned home.

The book is filled with Thoreau's observations of the shoreline and his reflections from the past. He never mentions his brother John by name, who died of lockjaw two and a half years after this river journey.

Thoreau paid for the first 1,000 printed copies, of which only 294 copies sold. He collected the remaining 706 copies and wrote in his journal, "I have now a library of nearly 900 volumes, over 700 of which I wrote myself."[1]

Concord River approaching the confluence

# An Eighth of an Inch

*"I have read that a descent of an eighth of an inch in a mile is sufficient to produce a flow"*

-Henry David Thoreau, A Week on the Concord and Merrimack Rivers, Concord River

This quote comes from the opening section of *A Week*, titled the Concord River. Thoreau describes the Concord as being "remarkable for the gentleness of its current, which is scarcely perceptible..."[2] He continues by saying, "Compared with the other tributaries of the Merrimack, it appears to have been properly named Musketaquid, or Meadow River, by the Indians. For the most part, it creeps through broad meadows, adorned with scattered oaks, where the cranberry is found in abundance, covering the ground like a moss-bed."[3]

I find two nuggets of wisdom in the quote. First, Thoreau enjoyed boating on the mellow flow of this broad, meadow river. The gentle current gave him an opportunity to slow down and explore nature's treasures more deeply. Second, he found intrinsic insights for life recognizing so little descent is needed to create a flow. I reflect on his second observation.

Look at how small an eighth of an inch is!

# *Oneness*

One eighth of an inch... It surprises me that such a seemingly trivial change in river descent would be enough to create a flow. How small, insignificant things can create major change. Like a small intrusive microbe called Covid-19 that we have grappled with these last few years. To see an image of this virus, it is unimaginable that such a tiny contagious germ could wreak havoc on the entire world, interrupting the flow of our daily lives.

One small microbe... One eighth of an inch...

The other day, hiking on a wooded trail near a pond teeming with the sweet song of Marsh Peepers, I crossed paths with a soft, brown, furry caterpillar. Soon, the caterpillar will molt into a chrysalis, eventually emerging as a butterfly, floating freely in a gentle breeze.

The little caterpillar reminded me of one of nature's phenomena called the "butterfly effect," where a tiny, localized change in a bigger, complex system can have large effects elsewhere. It is a term associated with chaos theory, where events in nature, such as a tornado, are influenced by the flapping of the wings of a distant butterfly several weeks earlier. It teaches us that a small change can influence bigger changes.[4] We are now on the brink of major, worldwide change. How will we each, as individuals, respond?

One butterfly... One small microbe... One eighth of an inch...

Kayaking has taught me insightful lessons over the years. In my second book, *A Season on the Water*, I reflected on my participation with a group cleaning up garbage along the Rock River. I wrote, "Paddling is the great equalizer, I've decided. I might be with the head of an international company, people who are retired, college students or stay-at-home Moms. No matter. It's all about sharing our love of being on the water. This is how life should be, I think to myself. We are all human, all trying to make our way during our time on this planet as best as we are able. Our judgments and evaluations of others, this emotional garbage, really have no place if we are to truly live a peaceful life." That day on the Rock River, we worked as individuals to clean up the residue and by doing so, collectively helped one another and nature.

One person in a little red boat... One butterfly... One small microbe... One eighth of an inch...

Pandemics and other catastrophic events also level the playing field. No one is immune. All of us must do our very best to protect ourselves and those we love.

We make a supreme effort to go with the flow of this unprecedented journey. One eighth of an inch at a time...

The virus has been with us for some time. One small microbe...

Small changes can have major impacts. One butterfly...

If each of us makes a small contribution we become part of the solution. One person in a little red boat...

During these challenging times, how do we come to terms with the paradox of these sweeping changes? In the midst of chaos, can we begin each day with a calm, quiet pause and ponder its meaning? Rivers continue to flow regardless of the depth of their descent or the obstacles in the way. Rivers swirl around and over impediments and sometimes through them.

Can we take some advice from the river?

I wrote this essay in 2021, yet the ripple effect from this pandemic still looms large in both harmful and helpful ways. These events remind us we are all spinning around together on our precious home called Earth and we are all responsible for doing our part to take care of each other and our planet.

If...

>...it only takes an eighth of an inch to create a flow in a river;
>...it only takes a tiny microbe to wreak havoc on our planet;
>...it only takes the flap of a tiny, butterflies' wings to evoke major change;
>...it only takes one person to point their boat in an open, positive direction...

...how much better will we be if we each paddle a gentle stroke? Toward goodness and kindness. And love.

Let us all begin bravely. Together.

*************

*What small step can you take today?*

*How would you feel if you knew your contribution, your eighth of an inch, made a difference in someone's life?*

*Can you keep your own life moving forward, ever so gently, against the headwind of major world events?*

17

18

# Decaying Tree

*"The decaying tree, while yet it lives, demands
sun, wind and rain no less than the green one.
It secretes sap and performs the functions of health.
If we choose, we may study the alburnum only.
The gnarled stump has as tender a bud as the sapling."*

-Henry David Thoreau, A Week on the Concord and
Merrimack Rivers, Sunday

This quote was written by Thoreau early in their trip on the Concord River. He and John stopped to rest on a sandy shore, and he was musing about writers, books and poetry. His reflections were a long sonata of bygone passages and a detailed commentary of writing styles.

I spent a long time reading and re-reading this quote, struggling to find meaning in the context of his contemplation about writers and books.

Perhaps it meant a decaying tree can still offer health benefits. He referred to the alburnum, which is the living, softer part of the wood between the inner bark and the heartwood.[5] In his next paragraph, he wrote about healthy books, which I saw as a nourishing correlation.

Growth from a decaying tree along the shore

19

## *Grief and Resilience*

About two and a half years after this river journey, Henry's brother, John, died in his arms, suffering a painful death from lockjaw. His brother's passing was one of the most tragic losses of Henry's life. *A Week* seems veiled in a shroud of incomprehensible grief.

So, I suppose it is appropriate to write about the decaying tree, its death and ultimately its hope for rebirth. Many times, on my paddling journeys, I see a partially submerged tree in the water, untethered from its roots on land. No longer a channel of nourishment for its leaves and branches, it lies limp along the shoreline. Rotting, moldy and decomposing. The gift of resilience trapped inside.

I have felt lifeless like this at times in my life, haven't you? Certain events or circumstances leave me feeling drooping, sagging and wilting my way through a day or longer. A waning interval of time exists between what was before and what is to come. A renewed sense of resilience is on its way, but how long do I have to wait?

I must admit, I have a deep interest in the journey of grief. I have experienced periods of time in my life where the anguish seemed unbearable. Grief, as I define it, is an unwelcome and unpredictable companion.

I have watched loved ones struggle with this agonizing challenge, wanting to bring comfort and shorten their painful path. If you know the joy of love, you know the ache of loss. The landscape has changed and there is no map to guide you.

Grief's itinerary is as individual as the loss itself. Unprocessed grief, I have come to believe, can be the most heart-wrenching of all. Let me share a story.

On one of our Red Kayak Institute retreats a woman came off the water after paddling for two hours in silence. During the sharing of what surfaced for her she began to sob and talk about the loss of her father. Her grief seemed acute as though his passing was recent, but she said he had been gone for 22 years. She cried uncontrollably. Her broken heart, trapped within a 22 year encasement of unprocessed grief, was splitting open. Heartbreaking to witness. Listening to her story tugged at my own memories of loss, uniting our hearts.

From my own travels with grief, I know on the other side, as I weave the grief into the tapestry of my life, healing and rebirth join the pain of loss and they move forward together. I begin a new journey, profoundly changed. The focus and the direction of my life shifts.

Just as we are intimate with individual grief, we also endure a broader, collective grief. All of us experience this in a different way as we witness and live through unsettling world events.

Henry wrote in his journal, on October 18, 1855, at age 38, "How much beauty in decay!" He is encouraging us to look deeply under the surface of sorrow, to find the joy patiently waiting at the bottom of the sea.

Within the slowly decaying remains of this tree, in the introductory pencil sketch of a dislodged tree trunk, life is teeming. New growth is sprouting and the decaying tree becomes an elaborate floating terrarium. Resilience is blossoming.

A landscaper, I think, would see this as a beautifully arranged composition. The taller, green reeds provide the backdrop for lower groundcover, or "log cover" as it would be. The addition of the lily pads floating in front of this waterscape add to the expansion of its beauty. Along

21

the backdrop of the bushy growth on the shoreline, this aquatic display makes me smile, and gives me hope.

In our world today, I feel we need hope more than ever. This decaying tree, this lesson of nature, shows us that within any seemingly unsettling occurrence, there is new birth. There is life. There is growth and there is color and joy and promise for the future. It comes to each of us in its own time, and collectively, we raise each other up.

"The constant abrasion and decay of our lives makes the soil of our future growth," Henry noted in *A Week*. "At any rate, our darkest grief has that bronze color of the moon eclipsed. There is no ill which may not be dissipated, like the dark, if you let in a stronger light upon it."[6]

We all need to find resilience, one of the greatest healers of grief. We spiral up, down, around and through the many cycles of grief, but somehow we remain steadfast. We maintain a buoyancy of spirit.

Let us embrace the decaying trees in our lives, and lean on them with the expectation of everything good and the optimism for faith in a brighter future.

Degeneration. Regeneration. Resilience. Hope.

*************

*Name a time when you felt like the decaying tree?*

*How did this interval of time make you feel?*

*What meaning did you find as this decaying tree began to sprout new life? And how have you carried this forward?*

# Thoreau

# Lapse of the River

*"...while we contemplated at our leisure the lapse of the river and of human life; and as that current, with its floating twigs and leaves, so did all things pass in review before us, while far away in cities and marts on this very stream, the old routine was preceding still."*

-Henry David Thoreau, *A Week on the Concord and Merrimack Rivers*, Monday

Henry and John are on the Merrimack River and they take a shoreline hiatus enjoying a snack of fresh melon in the shade of a deciduous tree. As they are casting away their melon seeds, Henry muses, "There are moments when all anxiety and stated toil are becalmed in the infinite leisure and repose of nature."[7]

He contemplates reform, politics and religion. He reflects on their impact on his own life and asks himself these questions: "What is that which a man 'hath to do?' What is 'action'? What are the 'settled functions'? What is a man's own religion, which is so much better than another's? What is 'man's own particular calling'? What are the duties which are appointed by one's birth?"[8]

This was a poignant interlude on the river with his brother, and one worth further exploration for us.

Pencil sketch from photo by Josette Songco of her dog, Daisy

25

# The Power of the Pause

Inhale.

On this quiet "spring" morning, the temperature is 42 degrees and I kayak onto the calm water for my first solo paddle of the season. Spring has made a slow approach this year, taking her time in the change of the season. As I write this, it is mid-April and the snow is flurrying, the ground snow-covered. Ice on the lake is intermittently interrupted by open water, 20 inches of ice to melt before the lake is completely open. Mother Nature at her finest!

I am fortunate to have open water along my shoreline leading to the river. I am anxious to experience my first paddle of the season, which gives me reason to pause.

During this interlude of the seasons there is much to take in. This is the time to inhale, internalizing all the gifts nature offers. This breathing space is my friend.

Why is this pause so important to me? Because I often feel so fragmented in my life. Don't you? We live in a hurried time where events are moving so quickly. We live with an unbearable sense of urgency, barely having time to process life's happenings before we are on to the next one. We unintentionally neglect to honor the space between an occurrence and a response.

As I kayak up river and observe the s-l-o-w-l-y changing season, my thoughts calm down. Even my heart rate drops a few beats. My breathing slows. This is healthy for me. A great morning for me to ponder a few of Henry's questions at the opening of this essay.

*"What is that which a man hath to do?"* Ahhh...our never-ending to-do lists. In this question, Henry is asking us to give serious thought to what is important. What really matters? For me, I place the emphasis on his word, *hath*, which is an old-fashioned form of the verb *have*. What is

it that we absolutely *have* to do? Deeper questions emerge for me as I paddle – are the things that I feel I *have* to do justifiable distractions? Do they keep me endlessly moving so I avoid taking the time to delve purposefully into my quiet space within? Am I camouflaging myself? I don't really know the answers. Sometimes deep questions lead to deeper questions. I make a journal entry to review my "to-do" list and make sure all these items are necessary. I also jot a note to be more mindful of what I continue to put on that list.

*"What is 'action'?"* A great pondering question this morning. Just as Henry sat and watched the twigs and leaves float by, I too watch the remnants of winter meander down the river – broken pine branches, smaller ice chunks and larger logs. Winter's debris is on the move. Action can be defined as movement. Isn't it interesting when you talk to people you ask them, "What did you do today?" as if being productive were the most important thing. Productivity has its place, but what about, "What did you feel today? What touched your heart deeply? What new thoughts stirred you?" Because another word for action is movement, and it doesn't necessarily mean physically. Reflecting and pondering my deeper truths I feel my inner terrain shifting.

*"What are the 'settled functions'?"* "Perform the settled functions," says Krishna in the Bhagavad Gita. "Action is preferable to inaction." Henry read the Bhagavad Gita and this Hindu belief reminded him that is was better to perform one's duties with no merit than to perform someone else's. I will continue to ponder this credence.

*"What is man's own particular calling?"* We each have our own gifts and talents to offer to the world. Often, it is too easy to get caught up in what others are doing, and think we should do the same. That is not *our* path, yet we let our fear of what others might think stop us. If Henry lived by the concerns of others, he would not be the

notable, quoted philosopher he is today. When given enough time to think and pause, we are awakened to our particular calling.

Many years ago, when my nephew Matt was in college, we completed a workbook together called, *What Color is Your Parachute?*. The book guided us through all areas of our lives helping us uncover our fulfilling, unique abilities while being of service to the world. We had a wonderful time identifying our talents as we came to know ourselves and each other in a deeper way.

Today on my paddle, I wrote a journal entry to pull out my notes from that workbook and review them. Sometimes, our pause on the river is all about reflecting on where we've been, deciding if changes need to be made and then keep paddlin' on.

Read the opening quote again. Henry is encouraging us to stop instead of bustling around in the same routines in the cities and marts. It takes time for the questions to enter our hearts, and even more time for the answers to present themselves.

Inhale.

*************

*Is everything on your "to-do" list necessary?*

*What is on your "to-be" list or your "to-become" list?*

*What is your own particular calling?*

# Fresh as a River

*"A man's life should be constantly as fresh as
this river. It should be the same channel
but a new water every instant."*

-Henry David Thoreau, A Week on the Concord and
Merrimack Rivers, Monday

Henry and John are still enjoying their rest on the banks of the Merrimack River. The previous essay about pause enabled him to ponder many thoughts, to take it all in, to watch life flow by. To inhale.

Thoreau was a deep thinker and this contemplative time opened his thinking about the freshness of this freely flowing river. The above quote was a reminder for him, and for us, to continually keep moving and keep our focus on letting go. This is our exhale. This is how we will stay fresh as this river.

Meandering White Sand Creek

# *Shedding*

Exhale.

This morning, as I enjoy my dark roast coffee and sit in the soft, filtered light of dawn, this quote about fresh as the river brings one word to mind: shedding. The ability to let go is hard for those of us who love to cling to deep, visceral things. Like the water, icebound under the frozen tundra, we are continually challenged to break out of our landlocked lives to stay open and fresh.

As I continue my reflection, open areas of water are slowly appearing on the lake's ice field. A white-tailed deer gingerly ambles toward an opening, and then continues on. The lake is shedding its ice and the deer must be vigilant as she prances along its tenuous edge.

Here in the Midwest, the winter has been relentless. I paddle on this spring afternoon as the ice is melting. I think about this season of change and the shedding of winter. I take to the river in my little red vessel where the water has been released from its snowy, icy covering.

The majestic bald eagle enjoys this time of year, keeping a close eye on the open, icy waters emerging from their frozen tomb. The warming temperatures are loosening their grip on this frozen lake, and the fish are abundant. The eagle recognizes this shift, and adjusts his food gathering patterns to the rhythm of this recurring cycle.

We, too, shift internally as the seasons change. Winter has been a time of hunkering down and allowing things to percolate within. Spring is the time of releasing, letting go of things that have been harboring in the deep dark of our inner world. Exhaling.

I start out on the icy shoreline and gently nudge myself onto the newly created water. I enjoy this transformative descent, dropping from the edge of the ice on to the

32

water. A rite of passage. I am reminded of the gentle poet Mark Nepo who wrote, "Transformation always involves the falling away of things we have relied on, and we are left with a feeling that the world as we know it is coming to an end, because it is."[9]

Where are the twists and turns of my life leading me?

I recently found myself craving solitude. A busy pace had been scraping away at the surface of my soul, my edginess a barometer indicating my need to step away. Simultaneously, I was also being pulled to spend time with significant people in my life, and I faced a choice. Do something for myself that I knew I needed, or share the gift of time with those I loved. I chose to be with others, the time was well spent and fun, yet I knew I had done myself a disservice. Two days later I found myself working hard to shed the frustration I felt, because I knew I had compromised a piece of myself with that decision. The barometer of edginess was still guiding my day. What was I deeply trying to shed? I discovered it was the inner conflict of honoring agreements with myself and honoring my commitment to others.

Life is a continual stream of shedding, letting go of what no longer serves us and discarding the mediocrity of the familiar. The grip of tiny tendrils can keep us captive in our comfort zone and hold us back from taking the next step. The shiny slivers of ice still clinging to the water's edge remind me that releasing unwanted and tired elements of our lives and in our hearts does not have to be a major task. Every small step we take in the direction of renewal opens a space inside to embrace the new.

Exhale.

With every seasonal shift, nature teaches us the importance of letting go. Effortlessly, she moves from one season to the next, releasing the outlived and embracing the new. I pass a floating feather resembling an angel's wing softly suspended in the air. The birds are shedding winter's coats. The feather drifts softly away on the water's surface. I sense a lightness watching this feather, a feeling that occurs when we unclog the stagnation and create a healthy flow in our lives.

Henry continues his reflections on this thought by writing, "Most men have no inclination, no rapids, no cascades, but marshes, and alligators, and miasma instead."[10] I don't want to stay in marshy stagnation, and I don't think you do either. Shedding is our way out into the freshness of the river.

As the radiant sun sets on this glorious paddling day, shimmering over open water and ice, I think about how nature has so many lessons to teach us if we are willing to learn. The transformation of one season to the next, the sunset of the evening and the sunrise of the new day, the ice melting and the water flowing. Nature is not afraid to change, to shed, to open the way for the new. Are we?

Exhale.

*************

*Are there things, people, circumstances, that appear beautiful on the surface, but are tarnished when you peer into the deep?*

*What do you need to let go of, if anything, to stay "fresh as a river?"*

*What is your shedding criteria? Make a list and let go!*

35

# Enveloped in Mist

*"Though we were enveloped in mist as usual, we trusted that there was a bright day behind it."*

-Henry David Thoreau, A Week on the Concord and Merrimack Rivers, Tuesday

Thoreau wrote this quote on the morning he and John set off on the Merrimack River after camping by a deep ravine near Penichook (Pennichuk) Brook, a salmon stream tributary of the Merrimack, near the town of Nashua, New Hampshire. The prior evening, they heated their cocoa, enjoyed dinner and talked of distant friends and the sights they were to see. As Thoreau wrote, "we lengthened out this meal, like old voyageurs, with our talk."[11] The brothers shared an intimate time. There were high winds that night, and violent storms elsewhere.

In the wee predawn hours, they hauled out their boat, packed it up, and by 3 a.m. they pushed into the fog, continuing on the Merrimack.

Kayaking in the morning mist

37

# *Trust*

In the still of the night, Henry and John heard the unexpected beating of a drum, intruding on the dark silence. The distant drumming caused Henry to stop his habitual thinking "as if the plough had suddenly run deeper in its furrow through the crust of the world."[12] Listening to the rhythmic beating of the drum, he remarks, "A strain of music reminds me of a passage of the Vedas, and I associate with it the idea of infinite remoteness, as well as of beauty and serenity, for to the senses that is farthest from us which addresses the greatest depth within us."[13] The Vedas are ancient Hindu scriptures recited or chanted during rituals.

"It teaches us again and again to trust the remotest and finest as the divinest instinct..."[14] His thoughts evoke deeper questions for me.

*What do I trust? Who do I trust? Do I trust myself? How do I trust the deeper instincts that reside in the depths of my soul?*

A little Q and A is in store for me as I kayak into the morning's pea soup fog, resting above the tranquil river's surface and rising to the muted spires of the forest green pine trees.

Weather forecast: A Dense Fog Advisory. Sunrise at 5:32am: Where? Too foggy to see. Temperature: 61 degrees. Wind: Calm. Conditions: Perfect.

A peaceful, mysterious aura emerges paddling in a foggy mist. These ground clouds blur the edges of the river and slowly soften the harsh contours of my thoughts. Although I am familiar with the bends and turns of this water route, the formlessness of the misty riverbanks challenges me to rely on my instincts. Limited visibility. Perfect for a lesson on trust.

38

Paddlin' on in my little red kayak, the twang of the green frogs and the low, guttural sounds of the bull frogs greet me. Welcoming the day and trusting I will not disturb their morning on the lily pads.

I hear a rustle, then a splash along the shore. As a wisp of fog drifts by, a white-tailed deer emerges, barely visible. I hear her munching on tree leaves along the riverbank. Breakfast! And then with assurance, she crosses the river, trusting I will not startle her. I drift along and dare not put my paddle in the water. I hold my breath, admiring her shadowy brown image as she steadily ambles to the other side.

Further up river, snorting sounds echo on the opposite river bank – the frisky river otter! Faint images of a dozen or so, popping their heads out of the water, looking around and then ducking under. Like playful periscopes! What do they see in this morning mist that is invisible to me? They trust that joy will be part of their day.

I paddle into a small section of lily pads and purple pickerel weed to eat my chocolate protein bar. I love having chocolate with me! My empty stomach is growling like a muffled bullfrog. Suddenly, I hear the *fwip-fwap* of bird's wings. Not just any bird, but the Great Blue Heron, majestically alighting from the shore in its prehistoric pose. She trusts her flight, knowing that above the low hanging fog, clear skies await.

The river appears broader in this morning's fog, expanding my thinking. I uncover the concealed answers floating in the veiled mist. These engaging creatures of river life have much to teach me about trust.

*What do I trust?* Like the frogs sitting contentedly on their lily pads, I trust I am exactly where I am supposed to be. To wish life would be any different is insanity. Frogs never hop backward, reminding me that when it is time to launch off my lily pad, I go forward.

*Who do I trust?* Like the deer obscured in the morning mist, I trust those who are sincerely interested in helping me cross the river. Those who are as deeply committed to my growth and happiness as I am to theirs. Those who sincerely share in my joys and sorrows, and those with whom I have no pretense. In the shadowy mist of uncertain times, we cross our rivers together.

*Do I trust myself?* Looking above and going below like the playful river otter, I continually challenge myself to monitor what is surfacing around me and what is bubbling within me. Underneath, I find my answers. Looking around, I see how they unfold, bringing me joy because I can say yes, I trust myself.

*How do I trust the deeper instincts that reside in the depths of my soul?* By taking flight, like the Great Blue Heron, even when the direction is unclear. By trusting in nature and a higher power to guide me. Those deeper instincts escort me on the flowing current of unlimited possibilities, the most important direction I can go.

Lift the misty veil. Trust.

*************

*What do you trust?*

*Who do you trust?*

*Do you trust yourself?*

*How do you trust the deeper instincts that reside in the depths of your soul?*

Paddlin'

40

41

# Thoreau

# Glistening Banks of Morning

*"We rowed for some hours between glistening banks*
*before the sun had dried the grass and leaves,*
*or the day had established its character.*
*Its serenity at last seemed the more profound*
*and secure for the denseness of the morning fog."*

-Henry David Thoreau, A Week on the Concord and
Merrimack Rivers, Tuesday

Henry and John continue up the Merrimack as the day brightens after the morning fog. Along the steep, clay banks, trickles of pure, cool water stream down into the river. This clean refreshing water is in contrast to the yellow and tepid river. Thoreau comments, "Some youthful spring, perchance, still empties with tinkling music into the oldest river..."[15]

Their course lay between the territories of Merrimack, on the west, and Litchfield, on the east. Along this stretch of the river their view was alternating wood and pasture lands, sometimes fields of corn, potatoes, rye or oats and in longer intervals, a farmer's house.

Soon, they caught sight of Mt. Uncannumuc rising before them to the west.

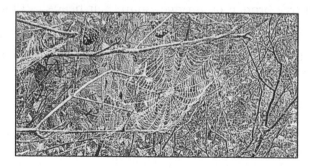

Pencil sketch from photo of the intricate spider's web

43

## *Awaken to Your Gifts*

I have been struggling to write this essay for some time and it always amazes me where the inspiration comes from to get my thoughts flowing.

This morning, I see a spider crawling on my bathroom floor and instantly, I think of the intricately woven spider webs I previously photographed along the river. I gently pick him up and put him outside.

A crisp 37 degree morning greets me at this hour after sunrise. I fill my coffee mug from my dear friend Jackie that says, "I'd rather by kayaking" and say out loud "You know it, Jackie!" The fresh aroma from the dark roasted coffee smells heavenly. I grab my camera and journal and off I go to the river.

This is my first solo paddle of the season. The veil of morning mist is lifting into the warm rays of the morning sun. The misty dewdrops left behind are glistening on the straw colored reeds and pale green lily pads gracing the shoreline. The intricate threads of a spider's web are shimmering as I had hoped and I pause to take a photo.

On the unfolding of this day, I am awakened to the beautiful gifts of nature. Three hungry deer munching on a tree branch on a ridge, snap their heads in unison to stare at me as I paddle by. A trio of beaver slap their tails on the water as I paddle near a new lodge they have constructed. The busy housing market is booming everywhere, I think to myself, and smile as I paddle on.

A bald eagle takes flight from a pine tree above me and the Mallard and Merganser ducks amble along the river's edge. The sights of nature's gifts greet me at every turn of the river this glistening morning.

I hear the loons' haunting tremolo call in the distance, and nearby, a chirping choir of Marsh Peepers serenade me, the little frogs heralding the arrival of spring. The sounds of nature's gifts fill the air.

I take a right turn into a narrow creek towards a little inlet a half mile in, perfect for journaling. I hear a cacophony of birds and am surprised at how the faint sound of my paddle in the water intrudes on their cheerful chorus.

I back into this small space, surrounded by sepia toned reeds, dewdrops shimmering on their emerging hints of green. I take a few long, slow sips of my robust coffee and let the morning sun warm me. Spring is beginning and all of nature is coming alive.

As I linger to ponder the dawning of this spring day, I feel blessed to have seen and heard so many gifts of nature in the first two hours of this paddle. Nature gives her gifts with unconditional love for us. They are free for the taking, and when we unwrap her packages, all our answers are inside. Henry knew this and I feel it, too.

How do I freely give my gifts and offer my talents? How can I best emulate nature's generosity? She gives, never asking for anything in return.

When I was a little girl, I loved to draw with a Spirograph, a geometrical drawing device enabling me to make detailed designs. It is with me now in my little red vessel with the intention to replicate the intricate spider's web. Can I reproduce one of nature's gifts?

In the small cockpit of my kayak, I have little room to maneuver the drawing board, so I lay it out on top of my boat and begin to draw. I choose a small wheel, which I put inside a larger wheel and rotate the gears around to make the shape. I used to be pretty good at this, but today, trying to duplicate a version of the spider's web, I fail miserably. I look at my drawing and I look at the photo I took of the spider's web and laugh. We are no match for nature.

Yet, we all have our own gifts and talents. When we show up every day with our unique artistry, presenting to the world what we, and we alone, can offer, we are replicating nature. Each one of us can awaken to the brilliance we alone can contribute freely, just as nature graces us with her blessings every day. I once read this quote by the Persian poet, Hafez, "Even after all this time, the sun never says to the earth, 'you owe me.' Look what happens with a love like that, it lights the whole sky." Nature never says that to us either. What a gift!

Paddling back, the bounty continues...a turtle on a log sunning himself, a jet black raven sitting high up on a barren branch of a tamarack tree eating a fish, hearing the trumpeter swans on a nearby lake and the *conk-la-ree* of the red-wing blackbirds, the heralds of spring.

Nature's gifts, both sight and sound, bring a sense of peace and calm to my spirit. As we all awaken and bring the universal gifts of love, kindness and compassion to the world, peace and calm will reside in our hearts.

*************

*What are your unique gifts and talents?*

*How are you bringing these abilities to the world?*

*At the end of every day, ask yourself this question – What have I done today, like nature, to bring peace and calm?*

# Thoreau

## Summiting Mt. Monadnock
### Jaffrey and Dublin, New Hampshire
### Elevation 3,165 Ft.
### September 27, 2022

1844-1860 - During this time, Thoreau summited Mt. Monadnock four times, and stayed overnight a few times on the summit. It was the mountain Henry cherished most. His journal entries also hint at the spiritual meaning the mountain had for him.

*As I prepare for my ascent, I write this note to carry, connecting Henry and me more deeply on this climb:*

---

Dear Henry,
I originally intended to hike Mt. Uncanoonuc in New Hampshire today, both North and South peaks. But after watching a YouTube video about the hike, the place looked unappealing to me, and you would have thought so, too. Run-down, collapsed buildings and the South peak loaded with cell towers. Ugh! Thankfully, I changed my route to hike here at Monadnock.

You wrote, "Those who climb to the peak of Monadnock have seen but little of the mountain. I came not to look *off from* it, but to look *at* it. The view of the pinnacle itself from the plateau below surpasses any view which you get from the summit."[16]

Today is September 27, 2022, and I hope to summit Monadnock. In the choice to switch to hike this mountain, I am wonderfully surprised to find that this was the one you loved most, and that you found spiritual meaning here. Being a spiritual seeker myself, I loved the fact that you summited here in 1858 with H.G.O. Blake, another spiritual seeker who was a friend of yours. The connection seems deeply serendipitous.

"There is a spiritual connection to Thoreau that I anticipate deeply on Monadnock. It is my quest for 'my own higher latitudes' and elevation of my purpose."                                    - Mary Anne Smrz

---

*On this sunny, 60 degree September day, Dee Beckmann and I drive to the area of Dublin and Jaffrey in southern New Hampshire to summit Mt. Monadnock.*

49

In geological terms, a monadnock is defined as "an isolated hill of bedrock standing conspicuously above the general level of the surrounding area." [17]

Mt. Monadnock is the exemplification of this description, sitting on the divide between two major watersheds, the Connecticut River to the east and the Merrimack River to the west. Without getting into too much geological detail, the rocks of Mt. Monadnock and much of the surrounding area of southern New Hampshire were once a layer of the sea floor. [18]

It is no surprise, then, that Henry wrote his thoughts about sauntering on the summit in his journal as follows, "It often reminded me of my walks on the beach, and suggested how much both depend for their sublimity upon solitude and dreariness. In both cases we feel the presence of some vast, titanic power." [19]

In this musing, Henry was sensing the spiritual aspects of this mountain. Of some divine power greater than himself. For as much as he loved the view from different vantage points of the summit, he loved looking at this mountain more. Perhaps these 400 million year old rocks, which jutted up from the sea, gave him both an unrecognizable, yet familiar, feeling of distant, ancient energy. In his journal, he wrote about the nighthawks, saying, "their dry and unmusical, yet supramundane and spirit-like, voices and sounds gave fit expression to this rocky mountain solitude. It struck the very key-note of the stern gray, barren solitude. It was a thrumming of the mountain's rocky chords." [20] For Henry, the timeworn, smooth granite rocks of Mt. Monadnock were alive with the perpetual spirit of primal forces.

A long introduction to this mountaintop for you, my reader! In many ways, it is important for me to capture the spiritual essence of this mountain. Perhaps, this is why Mt. Monadnock claims the notoriety of being the most climbed mountain in the United States, and second in the world to Mt. Fuji in Japan. [21] There is a deeper, intangible presence here, more than simply climbing the mountain for the physical challenge. Whether people recognize it or not.

Just ask Larry Davis, the 75+ year-old gentleman we met on our way up, who hikes the mountain two times each day, and was currently on his 6,029[th] climb. Amazing!

We begin our ascent at 9 a.m. up the clearly marked White Dot Trail. It is the shortest and steepest trail to the summit and it takes us 2.5 hours to reach the top. The slate-gray terrain we scramble over holds true to its description - large, smooth, granite boulders, briefly interrupted by smaller, jagged rocks.[22]

As we climb and I put my hands on the rocky incline, I feel the warmth and energy from this ancient stone. I read later that granite is often used for the healing benefits of hot stone massage because of its ability to hold heat for a long time. These old stones are embedded with fossilized wisdom.

The summit is a collection of these larger, granite boulders. The area is referred to as denuded, which means barren. The summit is bare because of fires set by early settlers in the region. The first, to clear the lower slopes for agriculture and the next, to rid the mountain of wolves they believed lived there.[23]

No summit sign greets us. Just high winds and beautiful vistas. Small areas where seafoam blue water has pooled in between the gull-wing gray slabs remind us of tide pools. We take a few pictures, including one of Monadnock's unique USGS disk marking its location in reference to five other peaks in the area. We hike down a short distance for a food break in a crevice below, sitting on the pewter gray rocks, warmed by the sunshine and protected from the blustery wind. Did Henry sit here, I wonder?

Lunch is our usual peanut butter sandwich, trail mix and protein bar. Henry's provisions, depending on the time of year he was here, consisted of freshly picked mountain *blueberries and cranberries along with these items he carried for his days and nights on the summit: "18 hard-boiled eggs, 2.5 pounds of sugar, salt, ¼ pound of tea, two pounds of hard bread, a half loaf of homemade bread and a piece of cake."[24] Quite a different sustenance!*

*We begin our trek down White Cross Trail, an easier but longer route. We are surprised by the beautiful little meadows that are discreetly and quietly tucked among the granite faces. As the sun shines on the fading colors of the remaining wildflowers of the season, I ponder the spirituality of this mountain. Did I experience any spiritual awakenings as I had hoped? Did I feel the ancient energy from the stone that Henry alluded to?*

*Pondering these questions during our 2.5 hour descent, these thoughts come to me. The rounded edges of the granite boulders that are our trail have a flow to them. A softness that in some ways seems calming, serene and peaceful. The tiny colorful wildflowers growing amidst the grayness and hardness remind me life can begin and flourish in trying and challenging situations. The distant mountain ranges and the sparkling lakes and ponds seen from the summit, beckon me to keep expanding my own vista. The mountain's barrenness encourages me to keep things simple. Life is easier and clearer that way. The roundness of this summit, with no real definitive peak, reminds me to enjoy the journeys of life as much as reaching the destinations.*

*These revelations make me smile, and I am grateful we hiked Henry's most cherished mountain today. In his honor, there is a Thoreau Trail and a low lying Thoreau Bog. His mark on this mountain remains.*

*Henry summited Mt. Monadnock four times. He spent a total of 11 days on the summit, traversing the pewter gray stone, cataloging the botany and geology and journaling his observations of the clouds and weather.*

*Henry hiked Mt. Monadnock on these occasions:*

1.  *July, 1844, age 27 by himself*
2.  *September 6-7, 1852, age 35 with Ellery Channing*
3.  *June 2-4, 1858, age 40 with Harrison (H.G.O.) Blake*
4.  *August 4-9, 1860, age 43 with Ellery Channing*[25]

*Mt. Monadnock in the distance*
*Pencil sketch from photo by Dee Beckmann*

# Thoreau

# Friendship

*"As I love nature, as I love singing birds and gleaming stubble, and flowing rivers, and morning and evening, and summer and winter, I love thee, my Friend."*

-Henry David Thoreau, A Week on the Concord and Merrimack Rivers, Wednesday

Henry and John stop for lunch after passing through the locks above the town of Amoskeag, New Hampshire, where the Merrimack River widens into a lake a mile or two wide. From the shoreline, they watch the canal boats go by, the sailors offering to tow them along.

These sailboats, however, moved sluggishly up the river, struggling in the non-existent breeze. After Henry and John watched the last boat go by, they launched their canoe and by the time they reached their evening resting place, they had passed all the slow-sailing boats.

When they were alone on the river, Henry wrote, "While we float here, far from that tributary stream on whose banks our Friends and kindred dwell, our thoughts, like the stars, come out of their horizons still;"[26] In my copy of *A Week*, he writes about friends for 25 pages.

Me in replica of Thoreau's cabin at Walden Pond
Pencil sketch from photo by Dee Beckman

## *Reciprocity*

The pencil sketch on the previous page is at the replica of Henry's cabin at Walden Pond. I am sitting at his desk, pretending to write. It is November of 2019.

I often set a plan for the upcoming year to consistently do something special. After sitting at his desk, I decide that in 2020, I will write a daily note to all the people I know. Do I really know 365 people? I will find out.

I print 365 cards, the picture of me at his desk on the front and inside, Henry's saying about friends - "Friends. They cherish one another's hopes. They are kind to one another's dreams."[27] I plan to write a handwritten note in each card every day.

I initially had many people who would receive my cards. But as the year went on, I found I had to search deeper for connections in my life. I ended up sending cards to my dentist, doctor, accountant, attorney and their administrative staff. I sent cards to friends of friends who would have never expected to hear from me. It was an amazing year and so very rewarding to realize there were so many fabulous people in my life. And I was pleasantly surprised at the number of handwritten notes I received back from people. Handwritten!

Friendship, like many things today, runs the risk of being cheapened. We live in a world of sound bites, short blurbs of information or contact and then on to what is next. Depth and meaning elude us. Handwritten notes have become an antiquated mode of communication.

Unknown to all of us at the beginning of 2020, the pandemic, Covid-19, was on its way to disrupt our lives and put us all into unwanted quarantine. Human contact was now dependent on Zoom, FaceTime or Skype, webinars and increased texting. Technology helped us through the endless isolation. My hand-written notes felt more intimate and provided more of a "human" touch then our phones or computers. Friendship took on a deeper meaning.

With Facebook, Twitter and others, it is easy to "friend" someone. And what does that really mean? Are these people we are "friending" really our friends? I think not. The word friend in this instance is shallow.

Not that technology is a bad thing. It is a way to keep in vital communication with those we care about. But in many ways, we have come to use it as a crutch, replacing voice and personal contact.

Henry loved his friends and deeply cherished those with whom he had reciprocity. He writes, "Friendship takes place between those who have an affinity for one another, and is a perfectly natural and inevitable result."[28]

I feel the same way. Reciprocity is defined as the practice of exchanging things with others for mutual benefit.[29] Interestingly, I learned that there are three types of reciprocity:

1. Generalized – giving without expecting a specific outcome
2. Balanced – equal give and take
3. Negative – unequal.[30]

I will take numbers one and two any day.

Henry writes, "But sometimes we are said to *love* another, that is, to stand in a true relation to him, so that we give the best to, and receive the best from, him."[31] This quote represents true reciprocity.

Another vital type of reciprocity is our intimate friendship with the natural world, our earthly home that is our space to find the eternal bond to our soul. Nature brings forth a harmony in our spirit and connects us to the divine. Nature gives us much more than we realize, and it is our inherent responsibility to give something back to her. To tend to her, with a reciprocity that expects nothing in return.

Henry also said, "Between whom there is hearty truth, there is love; and in proportion to our truthfulness and confidence in one another, our lives are divine and miraculous, and answer to our ideal."[32]

Let us have hearty truth and reciprocity with one another and with nature. That is what makes us whole.

*************

*Look at your friendships. As you look at each person in your life, what type of reciprocity exists between you?*

*Which friendships are truly reciprocal in a healthy way?*

*How can you cultivate more of those in your life so the divine and miraculous may unfold?*

59

# Tide of Circumstance

*"Our particular lives seem of such fortune and confident strength and durability as piers of solid rock thrown forward into the tide of circumstance. When every other path would fail, with singular and unerring confidence we advance on our particular course. What risks we run!"*

-Henry David Thoreau, A Week on the Concord and Merrimack Rivers, Wednesday

Up the Merrimack River near the town of Hooksett in New Hampshire, the brothers stop at a farmer's house to get provisions–home-made bread, musk and watermelon for dessert. They find their place to camp for the night at the mouth of a creek on the east shore, out of the way of passing boats on this busier stretch of river.

While eating dinner, Thoreau comments that the night is so serene, there are no words to describe it. He begins a late-night musing..." Our circumstances answer to our expectations and the demands of our natures. I am astonished at the singular pertinacity and endurance of our lives. The miracle is, that what is *is*, when it is so difficult, if not impossible, for anything else to be;"[33]

The secretive American Bittern

61

# *Choice*

On this glorious, sunny, 60-degree morning, I paddle up the Trout River from Wild Rice Lake in northern Wisconsin.

The thin stalks of wild rice sway in the slight breeze and the sun warms me, rising into the ethereal blue sky. I paddle around the twists and bends of this familiar river, reflecting back on my many river journeys here over the last 27 years and all the choices I have made in my life.

I look at the reeds standing tall, cattails on some. I look at the diversity of trees gracing the meandering river bank – evergreen, birch, maple – and many others I don't know. Some trees are healthy, others broken by storms, their weakened branches hanging low over the water. Observing the diversity along the shore, this thought occurs to me–nature stands in non-judgment.

I think about the "tide of circumstance" that nature endures with every season. Nature, in her ability to accept these circumstances without judgment, teaches me a valuable lesson.

The "tide of circumstance" laps upon my shore many times throughout my life. Some tides are inviting waves of goodness and happiness, others a stormy churning of unsettled and unwelcome swells.

Each presents me with a choice. How do I respond? What new decisions will emerge as a result of this gentle ripple or menacing storm surge? Like nature, can I stand in non-judgment of whatever may get deposited on my waterfront?

I find it challenging at times to accept the circumstances presenting themselves in my life. We all want things to unfold according to *our* plan, instead of making the choice to trust what the universe has in mind.

I paddle around another recognizable turn in the river and my kayak drifts a little closer to the reeds. There, standing unshaken by my presence, is a bird I have never seen before. It does not move and I paddle backwards not wanting to frighten it from its sentinel stance, guarding the reeds from unintended visitors, like me. I take its picture and continue on, leaving this tawny brown feathered sentry to its motionless, statue-like inhabitance.

Sometimes, when I am paddling and experience unique sightings like this, I think, "What are the chances that I would be here, in this time and place to see this bird, and what does it mean?" If anything.

After paddling another mile or so up river, I begin my journey back. At this same turn of the river, the bird is still there. It has not moved. Now I think, "Really, *why* am I seeing this unfamiliar bird again?"

I research the photo of this bird and learn it is an American Bittern. A rare, stocky, brown heron that is found in marshes and bogs, usually secretive and difficult to see.[34] It is barely visible in the photo at the beginning of this essay.

In a similar "tide of circumstance" I discover that one morning, Henry and his brother saw a bittern as they left their overnight stop, and he referred to this bird as the 'genius of the shore.' He comments, "It still lingers into our glaring summers, bravely supporting its fate without sympathy from man, as if it looked forward to some second advent of which *he* has no assurance."[35]

So now, I'm thinking about this bird. If he or she can look forward to something of which there is no assurance, can I? Learning more about the bittern, I discover "they are often found in an unusual rigid pose with neck outstretched and pointed to the sky. This is done to make use of the Bittern's impressive camouflage which allows it to disappear into the marshes. Encountering a bittern is a reminder not to fear the unknown. The Bittern reminds you to plunge into new situations with courage and optimism."[36]

I think about the adaptability and courage of this bird, the lesson of the morning for my thoughts on "tide of circumstance." No matter the tides, can I adapt and move forward with courage?

I want to make the conscious choice to do this. First, I look closely at my past choices, both good and bad, and honor them all. They have all led me on a beautiful life's journey bringing me to today.

Then, with clarity, I decide regardless of the "tide of circumstance" that will continue to visit my riverbank, I can choose my response. Like nature, I can non-judgmentally accept these conditions; like the bittern, I can trust without assurance, that whatever has landed on my shore is ultimately for my greater good. And adapt with courage. What risks we run!

*************

*What "tide of circumstance" is lapping on your shore?*

*If they are welcome waves, can you choose to appreciate their blessings and lessons?*

*If they are turbulent crests and swells, can you also choose to appreciate their blessings and lessons?*

64

66

# *Walden*
## Published August 9, 1854, Age 37

On December 24, 1841, at age 24, Thoreau wrote in his journal, "I want to go soon and live away by the pond, where I shall hear only the wind whispering among the trees. It will be success if I shall have left myself behind."

His thoughts became reality at Walden Pond, for two years, two months and two days from July 4, 1845 to September 6, 1847. He was 28 when he moved in. Ralph Waldo Emerson owned the land and let Thoreau use it for free. He spent a total of $28.12$^{1/2}$ for his materials, the labor his own. His 10'x15' dream cabin realized.

After eight handwritten drafts, *Walden* was finally published seven years after he left the pond. The demand was a mere 300 copies over the next 15 years.

Thoreau's universal messages in *Walden* resonate deeply: the individual's power to live a life with meaning; the importance of self-reliance over society's institutions; the goodness of humankind; and, the profound lessons one can learn from nature. Today, *Walden* has been published in over 1,000 editions and many foreign languages. The book is considered one of the great American classics.

Walden Pond

## *Preserve Your True Course*

*"I desire that there may be as many different persons in the world as possible; but I would have each one be very careful to find out and pursue his own way, and not his father's or his mother's or his neighbors instead...We may not arrive at our port within a calculable period, but we would preserve the true course."*

-Henry David Thoreau, Walden, Economy

Thoreau writes this quote after a conversation with a youth who inherited acreage and wanted to live as he did at Walden Pond. Thoreau's response is "I would not have any one adopt *my* mode of living on any account."[1]

Interesting these quotes would be part of his Economy section of *Walden*. He muses about how what is true for one person, could be true for a thousand, but he lays caution to this approach. He is adamant about each person pursuing his own path and making his living in his own way.

He continues, "Above all, as I have implied, the man who goes alone can start today; but he who travels with another must wait till that other is ready, and it may be a long time before they get off."[2]

Snowy banks preserving the river's course

69

## *Authenticity*

The pencil sketch for this essay is a meandering river, its snowy banks holding its course. A river is a wonderful metaphor for my thoughts on authenticity.

A quote from *A Course in Miracles* reads, "How could I recognize my own best interests if I don't know who I am?" This question illustrates the essence of Henry's thoughts on preserving our own course. How do we know where we are going, if we don't know who we are?

So how do we uncover who we are at the most submerged level? The critical starting point to defining our course is to clarify and live according to our deeply held values. A business colleague of mine once said, "When your values are clear, the decisions are easy."

Like the river, pulled by gravity as it flows, we are pulled in many directions by life's circumstances, people, and stuff we "should" do. We preserve our course by staying in alignment with our values.

So often I think about mine as I paddle around the bends of a meandering river. I prioritize these guideposts in the order of BE, DO, HAVE, a process I learned from another business colleague of mine. Who do I want to BE, in order to DO the things that are important to me, to HAVE a fulfilling life? BE always comes first. I hope this helps you find a process that works for you to discover and preserve your own true course.

Let me share my inherent values.

LOVE – of myself, others and life. BE open to the truths that emerge from deep love of self. DO my very best to be a loving person in all circumstances. HAVE a loving and truthful heart and soul.

70

PEACE OF MIND AND HEART - in the spirituality of nature. BE aware of deeper truths every day. DO live a deeply spiritual life so my heartbeat matches the heartbeat of the universe. HAVE my nature match nature.

HEALTH – clean and balanced eating; consistent exercise. BE in excellent health on all levels. DO a monthly evaluation of all four pillars – spiritual, emotional, physical, financial. HAVE a healthy regimen I can maintain.

SIMPLICITY – clear out inner and outer clutter. BE very diligent about keeping my life open and simple. DO continue to clear out the unnecessary. HAVE clarity and mindfulness.

MEANINGFUL PURPOSE – what do I exchange my life energy for? What has MEANING? BE the truth I want to see in the world. DO create the uncreated. HAVE willingness to do something with no guarantees.

JOY – what do I do for FUN? BE joyful and truthful. DO live as my heart is calling me to live. HAVE new and exciting adventures.

LEGACY – 100 years from now, how will people remember me? BE a writer. DO consistent plan for weekly writing. HAVE fulfillment and sustainability in building my life as a writer.

It has taken me a long time to identify the elements of BE, DO, HAVE that accompany my values. Am I 100% consistent in following these daily? Realistically, NO. But I write them down each year in my journal and refer to them often. They serve as guideposts to my authenticity, my true course.

Being mindful of my values also helps me set boundaries. Just like the river banks keep the water flowing in the direction that is true for the water, I too need boundaries to keep my life's flow on course.

Most of us spend more time planning a vacation or a party or a major life event than clarifying our values. But isn't the course of our life, living true to who we are, more important than anything? Identifying our values and knowing our purpose fuels our passion for life – beyond money and material wealth – and gives our lives meaning. How do we want to be remembered? Sometimes it is helpful to start this process from the end. What is our epitaph?

As I paddle on rivers, I observe how easily they flow, following their course. At a basic level, every river will BE uniquely shaped by elements, terrain and gravity; its dynamic water movement will DO what naturally occurs; and the river will HAVE a steady flow.

Unhappiness stems from actions inconsistent with who we are. I wish you the time and space to clarify your values to live your life from your authentic center. It is the most important thing you can do.

Be like the river. Preserve your own true course.

*************

*Before you continue, jot down five values on the next page.*

*How will you use these values to preserve your own true course?*

*Set a simple plan of action and get going. Right now.*

73

# Walden Pond, Day One
## November 27, 2019

This is my first visit to Concord, Massachusetts, Thoreau's birthplace and site of iconic Walden Pond, an appropriate place to begin. After a stop at the Concord Bookshop, where I buy a copy of his Journal, Dee and I get a bite to eat at the Main Streets Market & Café, filled with locals and tourists alike. Sitting at small tables positioned close together, we hear nearby conversations. The aromas wafting from the kitchen smell fabulous. I love being here, listening to the vibrant chatter about all things New England, so much of it about many of the great literary works of famous authors. My appetite is whetted, not only for breakfast, but for my visit to Walden Pond, birthplace of one of the great literary works by one of the greatest authors. The food is delicious, and soon we are paying the bill and are off to the pond.

"Excitement" is a very flimsy word to describe the butterflies in my stomach visiting this sacred ground. First stop is to the Walden Pond Visitors Center of course, to fill up a bag brimming with brochures, maps, and anything else I can get my hands on about Walden. We watch a movie about Thoreau and take pictures of a dozen displays, wanting to capture everything. The woman at the Visitors Center highlights the best path on the trail map, The Healthy Heart Trail, to hike around the pond. She gives me a free Thoreau bookmark, tells me about The Thoreau Society, and hands me a membership application. The Thoreau Society is the oldest and largest organization devoted to an American author. I join immediately. I pay for the purchase of my Walden Pond mug and dash out the door.

With trail map in hand and a spring in my step, I leave the Visitors Center. On the edge of the parking lot, before crossing the road to the pond, sits a replica of Thoreau's 10'x15' cabin. Inside is a staged version of the essential contents of his cabin - a bed, a desk, a table and three chairs- "one for solitude, two for friendship, three for society"[3] as

Henry described them. I feel his lingering presence here. Dee takes my picture at his desk.

Walden Pond is 61 acres, or 103 rods as they measured back then, in surface area. Its greatest depth is 102 feet, considered quite deep for a small pond.[4] The 1.7 mile trail begins to the right on Red Cross Beach and we follow the path to Thoreau's Cove and the original site of his cabin on the north edge of the pond. Nine stone pillars mark the outline of where his cabin stood. I enter the defined space. I hold my breath. I close my eyes. I am on sacred ground. I feel his love of solitude. I hear echoes of his words, "I went to the woods because I wished to live deliberately..."[5] I internalize his love of simplicity. I exhale. I stand there for a while, enjoying the grace of "being" in his space. I admire the beautiful view of the cove and walk the short distance to the water. It is peaceful there. The curve of the shoreline wraps around me. I feel safe. I feel calm. I feel at one with nature. I sit down on a stump. I never want to leave.

Hiking the remainder of the path around the pond, I am mindful with each step. Did Henry step here? Did he sit on a log like this by the water? Did he pull his boat to shore on Long Cove on the other side?

This contemplative state stays with me the remainder of the day, and that night I write in my journal, "I am looking forward to absorbing his insights and philosophies. I just love the gentleness of his ways. A man truly ahead of his time."

Thoreau's view of his cove at Walden Pond

76

# Where to Dwell?

*"What do we want to most dwell near to? Not to many men surely, the depot, the post-office, the bar-room, the meeting-house, the school-house, the grocery, Beacon Hill, or the Five Points, where men most congregate, but to the perennial source of our life..."*

-Henry David Thoreau, Walden, Solitude

Thoreau indicates in the paragraph including this quote, that some of his most pleasant hours were during long rain storms, when he was confined to his cabin. He was "soothed by their ceaseless roar and pelting" and felt that the longer span of time inside gave his thoughts time to "take root and unfold themselves."[6]

People frequently asked him if he was lonely there, especially on rainy days and nights. Thoreau wanted to reply, "This whole earth which we inhabit is but a point in space," and further comments, "Why should I feel lonely? Is not our planet in the Milky Way?"[7]

He was very content in his cabin at Walden Pond. His perfect dwelling place that connected him to his "perennial source of life."

Sign near the original site of Thoreau's cabin

# *Passion*

We are all born in a physical place on this earth – city, suburb, countryside, near the mountains, by a lake or an ocean and all places in between. Each has a distinctive tesserae - a look, a feeling, an energy - the intangibles that comprise its mosaic.

Many of us weave ourselves into this original tapestry and remain throughout our lives. Others leave for a while trying a new location of inspiration, only to return. And some leave never to come back, having found their "perennial source of life" elsewhere.

Wherever we go, or stay, the journey is ours. Henry wrote, "It matters not where or how far you travel,-the farther commonly the worse,-but how much alive you are."[8] Each of us finds our own place, our passion, our "perennial source of life."

What are we passionate about? How do we discover it? Do we have more than one? Let me share my story.

My passions have changed over the course of my life as I have changed. Many years ago, I owned a graphic design and marketing business. My entrepreneurial spirit was ignited every day with a passion for my work. I couldn't wait to get up in the morning and get to our shop and work long, tireless hours because the passion burned so deeply in me. I loved every element of this vocation. I loved the challenge of building something out of nothing. I had boundless energy and the inner joy of using my skills, creativity and talents. I wanted to do this forever.

After ten years in the business, a medical emergency landed me flat on my back. The universe had stopped me in my tracks and for the next six weeks, a "vacant endurance," as the poet John O'Donohue would say,

78

greeted me every day. The fast pace of building a business had come to a screeching halt.

When I emerged from my forced, contemplative sabbatical, I quickly realized I no longer had the fire in my gut to continue growing and running the business. The flame had been extinguished. My life's energy had been snuffed out. Within two years I sold the business and my life was headed in a new direction. But where? There was no passion to reignite me.

I found footing again in my career as a Certified Financial Planner®. I loved bringing value to my clients and guiding them on their financial journeys. I deeply treasured working with my business partner, Jason. The strict regulations of the financial services industry smoldered my flame somewhat, but working with Jason and my clients created the passion to keep my fire burning.

Many years later, kayaking in solitude brought healing to my broken heart after a string of personal losses. A deep passion, combined with purpose, surfaced. I knew it the moment I felt the excitement flare up within me. My solo kayaking excursions brought me healing, and I felt it could do the same for others.

I founded my own nonprofit, the Red Kayak Institute, to share the healing benefits of kayaking. And off I went with my new passion, my flame reignited on the water. I was hosting retreats for cancer survivors, grieving parents and women in 12-step programs. I designed a retreat to raise money for scholarship funds at a local high school. My passion was cresting high on the waves of bringing value in a new and meaningful way. I was again building something out of nothing and serving a higher purpose.

After eight years of providing healing on the water, our board decided to disband the institute. It was the right decision on many levels and we ended on a high cresting wave. But once again, my flame was extinguished.

And now? My passion is two-fold. The first is writing. Like building something out of nothing, the blank page beckons me. When writing, my thoughts flow from a higher source. Time evaporates. Not the boundless energy of passion running the business, the igniting sparks of the financial services work or the high cresting wave of the institute. A quiet passion. Something deeper now. A contentment of writing to bring value that will live on in perpetuity. An eternal flame.

The second, my life of outdoor passions. Kayaking, biking, hiking, and snowshoeing. Silent sports. Peaceful passions. Quiet time in nature.

Our passions change throughout our lives as we evolve and grow. And I know for sure when our passion, our "perennial source of life" is there, we *feel* it.

Even Henry, who loved his time at Walden Pond wrote, "I left the woods for as good a reason as I went there. Perhaps it seemed to me that I had several more lives to live, and could not spare any more time for that one."[9]

*************

*Where does your life gather its meaning?*

*What gives you endless energy and ignites your spirit?*

*What are you doing when time passes unnoticed?*

*Therein lies your passion.*

# Walden Pond, Day Two
## November 28, 2019

*Thanksgiving Day! How grateful is my heart to be on Thoreau's turf on this day dedicated to gratitude. We are only about an hour from Plymouth Rock, where the American origin of Thanksgiving was first celebrated in 1621, nearly 200 years before Henry's time. It feels so comforting to be surrounded by the richness of our history.*

*Today, it is back to the area surrounding Walden Pond. I stop to take a picture at the crossroads of Thoreau and Walden streets (yes, they actually exist) and we drive to Brister's Hill in Walden Woods.*

*A little background here. In July of 1846, when Henry was 29 years old, he was put in jail for failure to pay a poll tax. His reason was that the taxes would go toward the support of the Mexican-American War, which was expected to result in the expansion of slave territory. Henry did not support this, and his prison experience prompted him to write* Civil Disobedience. *Its central issue is how individuals peacefully respond when a government's policies are believed to be immoral. This issue still haunts us as a society today.* Civil Disobedience *inspired the likes of Mahatmas Gandhi and Martin Luther King Jr. who both believed in nonviolence.*

*Brister's Hill is named for Brister Freeman, a man born in Concord who spent 30 years of his life in slavery. He gained his freedom by serving in the Revolutionary War. Once emancipated, Freeman purchased acreage near Walden Woods. Henry spent time hiking and surveying here and Brister's Hill inspired his interest in forest succession. He wrote about Freeman and other slave families of Walden Woods in* Walden.

*Today, hiking Thoreau's Path on Brister's Hill, I am pondering the story and am not surprised he felt grounded here. A strong connection resonates with me, too. Along the one mile* path are sidewalk-gray granite slabs with Henry's inscribed quotes. This is one of my favorites, "I wish to speak a word for Nature, for absolute freedom and wildness, as contrasted with a freedom and culture merely civil, - to regard man as an inhabitant, or a part and parcel of Nature, rather than a member of society."[10]

Before we leave Walden Pond, Dee takes a picture of me next to a life sized statue of Thoreau. I put my arm around him. Me and Henry, simpatico!

Today was a day of history and gaining additional knowledge about Henry. After our hike, I insist we find "something turkey" to eat, since it was Thanksgiving after all. Of course, all the restaurants and grocery stores were closed in honor of the holiday. Finally, after searching for nearly an hour, we find a Dunkin'® and enjoy turkey sausage and egg bagels. Mission accomplished.

HDT and me!
Photo by Dee Beckmann

# The Earth's Eye

*"A lake is the landscape's most beautiful
and expressive feature. It is earth's eye; looking
into which the beholder measures the depth of his
own nature. The fluviatile trees next to the shore are the
slender eye-lashes which fringe it, and the wooded hills
and cliffs around are its overhanging brows."*

-Henry David Thoreau, Walden, The Ponds

Thoreau writes this quote about Walden Pond as he is journaling about the different aspects of this body of water. His time at Walden gave him a richer, deeper appreciation of lakeside life.

Walden Pond has no inlet or outlet so the water level rises with seasonal rainfall and lowers with the ultimate evaporation of the water. He notes the "shore is irregular enough not to be monotonous"[11] and observes the pond is "so remarkable in its depth and purity."[12]

Thoreau writes that the pond is "not very fertile in fish,"[13] the pickerel the most abundant and it "tolerates one annual loon."[14] He tells of companionable time with an old fisherman who arranged fishing lines seated by his cabin doorway and sometimes while sharing a boat.

Thoreau often fished by moonlight enjoying the night sounds of the fox and owls. On warm evenings he frequently sat in his boat playing the flute.

My cove sketch

85

# *Expression*

I love the tender way Henry describes Walden Pond in this quote. How the trees are the eyelashes and the hills and cliffs the overhanging brow. The lake, then, must be the face with all its myriad expressions.

I start today from my shoreline and paddle the half mile to one of the two islands that dot the face of my lake. One island has no access, save for the loons nesting there and the eagles perched high in the pine trees. The other island has a small entry slot where I land and hike the 20-30 feet to the top of this island. From this vantage point I can see the entire lake, complete with its own fringe of pine, birch and other trees, remnants of ice age boulders, stands of reeds, and of course, lakeside homes.

I slowly turn around in a circle to get a complete panoramic view. I pull out my copy of *Walden*, which I carry with me and read a few more of Henry's lines, "...Walden is a perfect forest mirror...a mirror which no stone can crack. A field of water betrays the spirit that is in the air."[15] As I survey my lake from the perch of the island, I wonder what spirit is lurking today.

A gentle spirit, I decide. The soft breeze is expressing itself, sending ripples across the surface. The gentleness of the wind evokes calmness. The lake, its aquamarine color reflecting the blue hue of the summer sky, is smiling. Happy to be basking in the warm summer sun and feeling the gentle breeze, just as I am.

I return to my little red kayak, patiently waiting for me in the slot, and push back out onto the lake. Now becoming so intimate with the water, its color changes. A gingerbread brown near the sandy shore, and a slate gray hue as I paddle over deeper waters. Just as we have many expressions during our day, I think to myself, so too, does the lake.

It expresses everything - the clouds, the sky, the sun, the moon, the trees and the shoreline shrubbery – eloquently conveying the surrounding beauty. It reflects my red kayak and my yellow paddle blades. And if I look down towards the water, it mirrors my smiling face!

I think about the many ways we express ourselves. We bring forth our creativity – drawing, painting, writing, photography, dancing, cooking, decorating and more. We communicate our compassion in helpful ways – teaching, volunteering, speaking, the healing arts and more. We are the full expression of our passions and interests.

I paddle near the boat landing, and I think of people having fun as they launch their vessels with joy– speedboats, jet skis and pontoons. And I think of people expressing a sense of calm while they are fishing or paddling like me.

I kayak over to a small cove not too far from the boat landing, and scan the natural landscape. I look at the facial expression of this cove – coconut-white and golden yellow lilies floating on the shimmering, shamrock-green leaves; reeds hugging the winding shoreline; small and large graphite-colored boulders dotting the shore; uprooted, partially submerged birch trees; and, tall pines framing the background. What a beautiful, expressive composition. I try my hand at a sketch of the reeds and lily pads. Not the best, but a little creative expression!

As I rest in my boat in this cove, I think about our own self-expression. When genuine, we are the best version of ourselves. We each have our own unique style to articulate our thoughts, feelings, opinions, and emotions. We use words, actions, facial expressions and body language to communicate our inner composition.

When we are joyful and happy, expressing our emotions comes easily. When we are sad, angry, upset or troubled, we tighten up. We would rather keep these emotions bottled up inside. I found a gentle way to give voice to my difficult emotions by saying, "let me share what is on my heart." Who could shut me out or get defensive when I am simply sharing?

As I leave the cove, I give thanks for the fullness of its natural beauty. I continue to paddle around the lake and think about how important it is to fully express ourselves. If we ever want to be seen, heard and valued as human beings, we need the outward expression of our innermost selves. All of it. We need to bring forth our beauty, let it stand in our cove with others, and be acknowledged for the full expression of all that we are.

As I conclude my journey around the perimeter of the lake, I think of the variety of ways the lake expresses itself to me, the many emotions it shares with me and cajoles from me. We enjoy a healthy relationship, me and the lake. We can both freely express ourselves. As Henry declared in his journal, "I should wither and dry up if it were not for lakes and rivers."[16] Me, too, Henry.

*************

*Are there parts of yourself that you've always wanted to express but were unable? How can you start?*

*Share something uncomfortable today. How did that make you feel?*

*Just for today, make a list of three things to express and get them out there!*

Paddlin'

# The Life in Us

*"The life in us is like the water in the river."*

-Henry David Thoreau, Walden, Conclusion

This quote begins the second to the last paragraph of *Walden*. The previous paragraph refers to the British Empire and the United States being "first-rate powers," and that "the government of the world I live in was not framed, like that of Britain, in after-dinner conversations over the wine."[17]

The passage after the river quote notes it was not always dry land where he dwells. Then he recounts the story of a bug that emerged from an applewood table which had stood in a farmer's kitchen for 60 years. He writes, "Who does not feel his faith in a resurrection and immortality strengthened by hearing of this?"[18]

Thoreau is summarizing a variety of thoughts. He encourages us to keep moving, to believe nothing can be stopped, like the bug in the wood. To stay awake to all our possibilities, like the water in the river.

He closes *Walden* with these words, "Only that day dawns to which we are awake. There is more day to dawn. The sun is but a morning star."[19]

Bug on a lily pad

91

# *Flow*

Panta Rhei...

I love this phrase. Sometimes, when things seem topsy turvy, I stop and say it. What is Panta Rhei, (pronounced pän-ˌtä-ˈrā)? Translated as "everything flows," this saying is one of the most famous philosophical quotes attributed to the Greek philosopher Heraclitus. He taught that the universe is in a constant state of becoming and change.[20]

The word flow signals an opening, a way to keep the "life in us" moving. Reminding me not to stay stagnant but to appreciate, welcome and flow with the continual changes in my life.

I have favorite podcasts. Two of them are by speakers who have a word that is a trademark for their work. VULNERABILITY is often attributed to Brene' Brown. Her 2010 TED talk on "The Power of Vulnerability" is one of the most viewed talks in the world.

The other speaker I frequently listen to is Tara Brach, who embraces radical compassion and uses the simple word RAIN as a mnemonic for her insightful teachings. R-RECOGNIZE what is happening; A-ALLOW life to be just as it is; I-INVESTIGATE with a gentle, curious attention and N-NURTURE with loving presence.

So on this morning's paddle out onto the flowing river, I whine to myself, "I want a word!" Taking a cue from Henry's quote that the life in us is like the water in the river, I choose FLOW. Perfect, in my mind for the essence of river paddling. Everything flows. Panta Rhei.

F- FORGET. The first breath of *ahhhh* I exhale pushing off from shore helps me to release and let go of everything happening in my life on land. I make a conscious decision to free my mind from land limitations and let my thoughts FLOW.

L-LISTEN to the sounds of nature. The birds are chirping and singing. A slight breeze rustles through the trees and I hear the gentle quaking of the aspens' leaves and the soft *swoosh* of the wind moving through the pines. Most importantly, I LISTEN to a tender subtle silence that is woven into the sounds of nature, like the interval between notes on a musical scale. Just as the music is in the silence between the notes, so nature's deepest sounds are in the silence between our feathered friends' chorus and the breath of air caressing the trees. I bask in its welcoming embrace.

O-OBSERVE the sights around me. The way the rising sun sends its shafts of morning light through the shadows of the pines. The way the current on the river parts around jutting rocks and partially submerged logs, flowing around these obstacles. The way lily pads sway on the water's surface. The way tiny water bugs scatter in V-shaped unison as I approach in my little red kayak.

W-WILLING. From my time of forgetting, listening and observing on the water, I must then be WILLING to take what I have learned from my time on the river, and connect it back to my life. To keep the life in me invigorated like the current in the river.

What did this element of flowing water and its surrounding companions teach me this morning? This menagerie of river life reminded me of the ever-flowing stream of life. To continue to embrace and accept the changes and glide with the currents.

Everything is moving, evolving, emerging. A river is always changing, always in flux, just as we are.

The full Panta Rhei quote by Heraclitus ends with "...kai ouden menei," which means nothing stays.[21]

"The life in us is like the water in the river."[22] writes Henry. Let us be mindful to keep our lives fluid in our thoughts, actions and in our care for one another and nature.

Everything flows. Panta Rhei.

Nothing stays. Kai ouden menei.

*************

*What do you need to FORGET, to open your mind and heart to the new?*

*How can you do a better job of LISTENING and OBSERVING to uncover what lies under the surface?*

*What are you WILLING to do today, to open the FLOW in your life?*

# Thoreau

## Camp 19 - My Walden without the Pond
### July 30, 2022

*Thoreau opens his Solitude section in* Walden *with this quote, "This is a delicious evening, when the whole body is one sense, and imbibes delight through every pore."[23] I feel this same sensation on this cool, July evening as I begin my overnight stay at Camp 19.*

*Set back in the woods of my dear friends Sandy and Parker's property, is the sweetest 10'x12' cabin. Parker built this cabin during the Covid-19 lockdown, thus its fitting name.*

*Knowing I am writing about Thoreau, they offer me the gift of an overnight stay at Camp 19. I jump at the chance!*

*Our evening begins with "valet service" in Parker's UTV out to the cabin. Sandy's sister, Sue, joins us for our dinner fare of steak, baked potatoes and fresh-picked corn on the cob on the campfire, along with fruit salad. A VERY delicious start to the evening.*

*After evening conversation, they leave me to my solitude. As the vanishing sound of the UTV echoes in the distance, Thoreau's words echo in the silence, "Simplify! Simplify!"[24]*

*I am utterly alone and I embrace nature's sanctuary of stillness. I walk the narrow path in the woods a short distance, thinking of how deeply this experience at Camp 19 reinforces the refreshing life of simplicity. I gently touch the rough, brown bark of the pine trees, feeling the warmth of their calming energy. I hold a tiny rock in my hand, perhaps a piece of a larger glacial boulder. Once a part of something larger than itself. I pick up a pine cone, smelling its fragrance and wondering how it will regenerate itself.*

*How little we need! How much natural beauty to appreciate when rendered void of material goods. How delicious the silence when no words are spoken.*

*I sit outside in the utter stillness and warm texture of the last hour of dwindling daylight before I venture in.*

*The sparse interior of the cabin enhances my love of the virtues of simplicity. A small log bed, a wooden chair in the corner, shelves Parker built to hold essential supplies and a tiny, built in counter to hold the cook stove.*

*Henry would be proud! He might comment, as he did in Walden, "...for a man is rich in proportion to the number of things which he can afford to let alone."[25] I embrace the richness of the uncomplicated energy of this rustic cabin.*

*As darkness falls, I curl up under the woolen cover on the bed, pull out my flashlight and read passages from a book called,* The Illuminated Walden, *a gift from my cousins Steve and Diane. The visually invigorating photographs and Henry's insightful passages heighten my solitude experience of the Walden mindset. A cool soft breeze floats in to the cabin through the tiny, narrow windows. After a short while of feeding my mind with Henry's wisdom, I drift into peaceful slumber.*

*At 2 a.m. I awaken to the haunting call of the loon in the distance. A nearby "who cooks for you?" hoot of a barred owl summons. Unseen in the night, camouflaged by its mottled brown and white feathers, it softly voices its presence.*

*The mysteriousness of the pitch black woods beckons me and I emerge from the cabin to gaze at the star-filled sky. The immensity of the sky's vastness overtakes me, and I am graced with a shooting star. Henry wrote in his journal, "Shooting stars are but fireflies of the firmament."[26] I am standing under the dazzling umbrella of the pulsating life of the universe. I am so small. I am at peace. I inhale the aroma of eternity. I never want to exhale.*

*After a time, I reluctantly head back inside my rustic abode and fall fast asleep.*

*I arise at 5 a.m. greeted by the nasal call of a Red-breasted Nuthatch. I grab my army green Stanley® thermos of coffee and sit on the primitive log bench on the porch, which faces east. The first golden aura of light streams through the pines. I do not journal or read. I quietly immerse myself in the unfolding of the day. Thoreau wrote in* Walden, *"All memorable events, I should say, transpire in morning time and in a morning atmosphere."*[27]

*Henry's cabin at Walden comes into my mind, and as I sit and "be" with the morning, I wonder what he thought each day as he stepped out his door. I look out at the woods and the mossy tree stumps along the pine needle laden path to the cabin. This delicious slice of solitude in the woods is reconnecting me to nature in a profound way.*

*I think of how this experience shaped Thoreau after two years, two months and two days of living this way. I begin to understand, during that stretch of time at his cabin, how Henry could sit and ponder for hours. He wrote, "I love a broad margin to my life. Sometimes, in a summer morning, having taken my accustomed bath, I sat in my sunny doorway from sunrise till noon, rapt in a revery, amidst the pines and hickories and sumachs, in undisturbed solitude and stillness..."*[28]

*Another hour of absolute quiet passes and as the sun gets higher in the sky, the soft tangerine orange light of the morning begins to brighten. Suddenly, a lone bumble bee buzzes around the cabin porch breaking the sacred silence. A signal to get moving on the day.*

*This solitary morning in the unsurpassed silence, the timelessness of Henry's quote in* Walden *echoes through the pines. "Every morning was a cheerful invitation to make my life of equal simplicity, and I may say innocence, with Nature herself."*[29] *I gratefully accepted that invitation today.*

*I text Sandy and Parker about our breakfast plans and soon they arrive with a bowl of pancake batter mixed with freshly*

99

picked blueberries and a side of bacon to complete our campfire feast. Katie, their sweet Irish setter, comes along to join us. Just as delicious as last evening began, so the morning meal nourishes our bodies and our deepening friendship feeds our souls.

After breakfast and meaningful conversation around the dwindling campfire, my Walden experience is complete.

In his journal, Henry wrote, "I feel the necessity of deepening the stream of my life; I must cultivate privacy."[30]

I am grateful to Sandy and Parker for this respite of solitude to deepen my stream. A much-needed turning point that has reignited my writing.

Pencil sketch from photo of Camp 19

# The Maine Woods
### Originally Published Posthumously on August 9, 1864

After Thoreau's death in 1862, his sister, Sophia and his frequent traveling companion, Ellery Channing, organized and edited his manuscript and published *The Maine Woods* two years later.

Thoreau went to the Maine woods three times, in 1846, 1853 and 1857, between his ages 29 and 40. Each of the three chapters in *The Maine Woods* designates one of his trips. On every journey, he climbed mountains, canoed rivers and lakes and made detailed observations about the flora, fauna, landscape, and waterways. He loved to listen to the folklore of his Penobscot guide, Joe Polis.

He loved the wildness and primitiveness of Maine, writing, "What is most striking in the Maine wilderness is the continuousness of the forest, with few open intervals or glades than you had imagined."[1]

His Maine explorations and discoveries were both interior, revealing his own adventurous spirit, and exterior, capturing the wilder side of America.

Mt. Kineo on Moosehead Lake

# Voyage of Discovery

*"While it is river, you will not easily forget which way is up stream; but when you enter a lake, the river is completely lost, and you scan the distant shores in vain to find where it comes in. A stranger is, for the time at least, lost, and must set about a voyage of discovery first of all to find the river."*

-Henry David Thoreau, The Maine Woods, Ktaadn

Thoreau and his entourage paddled on the West Branch of the Penobscot River, about 30 miles from the base of Mt. Ktaadn (Mt. Katahdin today). They stopped at a logger's camp to have their dinner. Being a warm evening, they decided to canoe by moonlight, reaching the vast 3,000-acre North Twin Lake by sundown.

The Penobscot River runs through North Twin and only one member of the party, George McCauslin, had previously crossed the lake to the other end of the river. Thoreau and company were fortunate. Having a companion who could recognize the far entrance into the Penobscot was a blessing, and at nine o'clock they reached their river campsite for the night.

The guiding light of the moon

# *Recognition et al.*

Crafting this essay has been a true voyage of discovery for me. Initially, I struggled to discern a meaningful message. I read and re-read the quote and the passage. Here is my discovery.

This is Henry's first trip to the wildness and unfamiliar territory of Maine. His goal to summit Mount Ktaadn is in his sights. Although there was a planned route, he was paddling unfamiliar waters.

They have been canoeing all day, are tired, land at an old logger's camp to have their dinner and then continue on. They leave late afternoon, venture another mile on the Penobscot River before reaching this large, looming lake at sundown. They paddle across the lake by the light of the moon.

I have kayaked a number of times in the moonlight. A full moon illuminates a lake, but the experience is wildly unfamiliar. My senses feel distorted and the inability to clearly recognize the faint outline of the shore is unsettling. I realize it does not take much for me to get turned around and confused locating my shoreline.

The first accolade for Henry on this night, was he RECOGNIZED he had no idea where to find the opening of the river on the other side of this lake. He realized he had to trust McCauslin's knowledge and experience.

We like to be RECOGNIZED, too. Not only for the things we do that are beneficial to others, but for who we are. It is a warm feeling when someone notices us and affirms us in meaningful ways. When someone "sees" us, we feel treasured and valued.

This recognition for Henry led to APPRECIATION. He appreciated his friend for the attentive care he gave to everyone, ensuring safe passage across the lake. While paddling, McCauslin kept everyone buoyant in spirit singing boating songs. Henry valued McCauslin, writing, "We could not but confess the importance of a pilot on these waters."[2]

Just below self-actualization on the fourth level of Maslow's Hierarchy of Needs is APPRECIATION. It is a fundamental human need. Being appreciated we feel respected and more positive about ourselves and our relationships with others. Appreciating people lifts them up and helps to increase their sense of self-worth.

Henry's appreciation of McCauslin escalated to GRATITUDE when they safely reached shore for the night. McCauslin had camped here before and knew there was a "...rill which would supply us with cool water emptying into the lake."[3] This safe harbor was a welcome camping ground for the weary travelers.

GRATITUDE is a tender virtue. We feel an affirmation of all good things within us, within others and in the world. Gratefulness is a warm balm enveloping us. Gratitude can be a stepping stone, giving us hope for good things to come. The more we manifest the positive benefits of being thankful, the more will be returned to us.

Finally, after the group landed on shore, their sense of CONNECTION was immediately evident. As a cohesive team, they worked to build a campfire. Some scoured for dead trees and branches, others cut fallen trees and boughs while others arranged the wood and started the fire. They had completed a challenging lake crossing together and the camaraderie was in high pitch.

CONNECTION tethers us to something larger than ourselves. It's the embracing feeling of "we are all in this together." We have varying degrees of connection with people. Those we are more tightly aligned with share our deeper values and are as equally committed to the nourishment and enhancement of our personal growth and happiness as we are to theirs. We also have different levels of affinity to family, friends, co-workers, teammates, neighbors and others. What we know for sure is we humans need the bonding, the connection to others. We need people we feel comfortable around, with whom we enjoy time and with whom we can be ourselves.

The next day, Henry and company canoed through lakes, poled up rapids, portaged around waterfalls, clambered uphill around endless rocks and logs and were challenged by fierce and fast rapids. But they made it to what I believe today is Abol Stream and the base of Mount Katahdin. After trout fishing that evening, they rested for the night and began their ascent of the highest mountain in Maine the following morning. "Here it fell to my lot, as the oldest mountain-climber," Henry wrote, "to take the lead."[4] And the cycle begins again.

My voyage of discovery is complete, revealing the gifts of:

RECOGNITION. APPRECIATION. GRATITUDE. CONNECTION.

*************

*On a daily basis, how can you make a more conscious effort to recognize and appreciate all the good in your life?*

*What feelings of gratitude can you show to others? Every day, can you write down three things you are grateful for?*

*How can you devote more attention to honoring the treasured connections in your life?*

106

108

# Where Will You Go?

*"In shooting the rapids, the boatman has this problem
to solve; to choose a circuitous and safe course amid
a thousand sunken rocks, scattered over a quarter
or half a mile, at the same time that he is
moving steadily on at the rate of fifteen miles
an hour, Stop he cannot; the only question is,
where will he go?"*

-Henry David Thoreau, The Maine Woods, Ktaadn

Thoreau was forced to abandon his attempt to summit
Mt. Ktaadn (Mt. Katahdin today.) He was hampered by
fog and misty conditions near the top. Although there
was no trail, his notes indicate to me that he hiked down
what is now the Abol Trail.

He and his companions got back in their canoes and
continued on the West Branch of the Penobscot River
until they came to Abol Falls, or what Thoreau notes
Aboljacarmegus Falls. The river leading up the falls was
full of submerged and jutting rocks, and Thoreau
mentions this section of the river presented more danger.

Their precarious journey continued until they carried
their canoes around Pockwockomus Falls and camped
overnight. The next day they ran more rapids until they
came to Quakish Lake, and quietly floated.

"Eagle Falls" at Fish Trap Dam
Photo by Dee Beckmann

109

## Destination: YOU!

I have a saying that helps me keep a positive focus in my relationships. That is, "We are all here to help walk each other home." What do I mean by that?

When we are born, we are whole, complete, untarnished by the world, unaffected by the emotions and opinions of others, undaunted about what others think and at peace. Doesn't that sound like a great place to be?

As we grow up, we are influenced by people, events, life's circumstances and what we think we should or shouldn't be doing. Before we know it, our unbroken self is splintered and we find ourselves navigating the uncharted waters of who we have become. Many of us have drifted far away from that newborn wholeness.

Our life's journey is to travel back to that destination of the true essence of who we are. How do we navigate?

In this passage Henry refers to the dangers of the rocks and the swiftness of the rapids. One mistake could send them overboard into the swirling eddies of the river. The boatman in charge must stay focused in the present.

This morning, as I paddle up the river, calm as glass, I peacefully observe and listen. The slant of the morning sun shines on the tall reeds. The brown cigar-like ends of the cattails sway gently above them. The dazzling, blinding white of the birch tree's bark reflects on the soft ripples of the water. The symphony of the morning birds welcomes the day. I am in the present moment.

In a March 27, 1848, letter to his friend, H.G.O. Blake, Henry wrote, "I live in the present. I only remember the past-and anticipate the future."

In order to "walk ourselves home" we, too, begin in the present moment envisioning the future version of ourselves. I recently listened to a podcast by Justin Michael Williams on Intention Setting. I do not set goals anymore, just intentions. Goals are great, but I think they can be limiting. Once we achieve them, then what? Intentions are more expansive, more fluid for me. They are more about who I want to become and how I want to feel, rather than what I want to achieve.

Anyway, Justin indicates a statistic that over 40% of our daily actions are not conscious decisions, but habits. To me that means almost half of our day is spent in rote, habitual action. Does that lead us anywhere? We unintentionally send ourselves overboard, swirling in the eddies behind the rocks, going nowhere.

In his podcast, Justin asks this question, "What energy do you need to cultivate more of in your life, *today*, *now*, to become that person you are seeing in that vision?" I answered with three words – peaceful, calm and tender. My path toward wholeness.

We will have different answers. Joy. Contentment. Gratitude. Kindness. Compassion. Empathy. Love. These responses are heart-warming. No negative answers here. Fear. Anger. Greed. Bitterness. We would not choose those, and yet they are so prevalent today.

Our thoughts about our future self, create a different picture for each of us. It is one of the beautiful aspects of life, how different we all are. On the river as I observe the flora and fauna on the banks, each bud, each flower, each leaf, each branch is different. Nature lives in harmony with each unique element. If we remove ourselves from internalizing the influences and expectations of others, we too, can live harmoniously with others while content in our own individuality. We all have something uniquely ours to offer to the world.

111

The future self's time frame, if you will, is also different. I am 67 years old. More of the arc of my life is behind me than ahead of me, so I better take a good hard look at my future self. She will arrive before I know it! Those of you who are considerably younger or older will have different durations, either extending over a longer period of time, or arriving very quickly.

In any scenario, creating the future vision of ourselves in the direction of being peaceful, kind, gentle and loving is universal. We can all share those. No matter what our life circumstances, occupation, age, etc., our destination is the same – wholeness, peacefulness, joy, harmony. It is our path to "walk each other home."

I close with this quote from Henry: "You must live in the present, launch yourself on every wave, find your eternity in each moment. Take any other course, and life will be a succession of regrets. There is no world for the penitent and regretful."[5]

Destination: YOU!

************

*Ask yourself how you want to feel today. Live that answer, just for the day.*

*The present moment allows us to recalibrate. How can you find more present moments in your day?*

*Answer Justin's question: What energy do you need to cultivate more of TODAY, NOW, to become the person you are seeing in that vision? Embrace it. Destination: YOU!*

## Summiting Mt. Megunticook
### Camden Hills State Park, Camden, Maine
### Elevation 1,385 feet
### October 1, 2021

*On his trip to Maine in September, 1853, at age 36, Henry left Boston on a steamer ship for Bangor, Maine, going the outside course. As he came up the ocean through Midcoast Maine, Henry commented, "Next I remember that the Camden Hills attracted my eyes..."[6]*

*Henry's eye probably caught sight of Mt. Megunticook, the highest peak in Camden Hills State Park. Although he never hiked here, on this stunning fall day, with temperatures in the 60's, Dee and I head for this summit.*

*Megunticook is a Penobscot Indian word referring to the swelling ocean and probably named that way because the Atlantic Ocean laps right up to the base of this mountain.*

*We begin the steady climb to the summit. The impressive trail is rugged and rocky. We tramp across the boardwalk over low lying areas and trudge around rocks surrounded by large, twisted tree roots. We take pictures next to old growth trees, with pale orange and yellow mushrooms encircling the peeling bark like a twisted vine.*

*When we reach the granite patches at the Ocean Lookout, the panoramic views of Penobscot Bay are stunning. Deep, cobalt blue ocean surrounded by rocky cliffs and luscious, green woodlands are a feast for the eyes.*

*We stay here before continuing to the summit to have our own feast of peanut butter sandwiches, peanut butter filled pretzels and trail mix.*

*We sit on the warm slate gray rocks in silence. The view speaks volumes and no other words are necessary. I wonder if this is the mountain that caught Henry's eye. From*

115

somewhere out there, he noticed this place. Back then, I would wave to him and hope he would see me and wave back.

After our lunch and rest, we head to the top. The true summit of Megunticook has no panoramic view, but it is essential to say we summited. Trees surround the giant rock cairn marking the peak. We take our picture, put a rock on the cairn and begin our descent, continuing to stop along the way to take in the expansive ocean views.

It was a visually invigorating, soul-filling and physically rewarding 4.8 mile hike. After a mouthwatering seafood dinner in Rockland, we walk down to the harbor, savoring the peacefulness as we watch the red-orange ball of sun sink into Penobscot Bay. A beautiful completion to the day and a toast to my Dad, who would have been 94 today.

*Summit of Mt. Megunticook*
*Photo by Dee Beckmann*

# McGee Island
## St. George, Maine
### October 2-9, 2021

*The next day, we drive to Port Clyde, a small fishing village on the edge of a peninsula, where my next adventure begins. Dee drops me off on the dock, cup of coffee in hand and bags packed at my side. I am off to the Salty Quill Writers Retreat for Women to spend a week on McGee Island.*

*My tugboat pick up is not for two hours, so I sit in the Adirondack chair on the pier, gaze out at the vastness of the ocean and think about my plans to begin organizing this book at the retreat.*

*After a time, I feel a bit chilled, so I head into the Port Clyde General Store, a sweet, local gathering place with a conglomeration of everything you could imagine for sale. There is a wooden counter where I sit on a stool and order a bowl of chowda. It warms me, and I relish the salty, rich texture of this place. Watching the locals come and go and listening to the conversations of the fishermen adds spice to the savory flavor of my chowda.*

*I head back to the dock, and soon notice fellow retreaters arriving and Joe, the captain of our tugboat for the 3-mile ride to the island, ties up to the dock. Soon, we'll be chugging out to sea to our island writing destination.*

*McGee Island, as best as my research tells me, is one of 50 St. George's Islands. Although Thoreau never went to McGee, he came through this area on the same 1853 trip to Bangor. He wrote in* The Maine Woods, *"The first land we make is Monhegan Island, before dawn, and next St. George's Islands, seeing two or three lights."[7] Monhegan is approximately ten miles from McGee, so he inevitably sailed near these waters.*

*It is fitting for me to begin the initial step of this book out here on this 110-acre island. As we bump along the waves to*

117

*McGee, I feel the salty spray on my face. I love that. There is something about the smell of the salty air and the taste when I smack my lips that seeps of times gone by. Did Henry have similar sensations of smell and taste on this same water as he sailed by?*

*We arrive at McGee and transfer ourselves and our belongings to a small row boat to tender in to shore. I step on the unfamiliar terrain of the Maine wildness Henry loved.*

*McGee Island is a private island nestled next to undeveloped Barter Island. McGee has three residential structures. The Main House, where we stayed, was built between 1913 and 1915. Quintessential weathered gray New England clapboard siding, wrap around porch, an outdoor shower and a large, living room with stone fireplace. Warm and welcoming.*

*The Cook House, the site of all of our fabulous meals by our cook, Erin, and I mean FABULOUS, was built in the late 1700's. This building also has living quarters, a quaint kitchen and a room filled from one end to the other with a large harvest table. Hungry or not, we couldn't wait to gather for every feast Erin cooked up for us.*

*The Little Boat House, built around 1915, sits at water's edge. I guess what building doesn't on a small island? It has living accommodations and a cozy seaside porch.*

*To compliment the outstanding living accommodations and gathering places, the island itself is graced with beauty. Rocky coves and beaches to launch our kayaks and paddle around the island. Hiking paths amidst the fields and forest, all surrounded by the glistening Atlantic Ocean. A place that steps back in time, where I could stay forever.*

*The Salty Quill Writers Retreat for Women beckoned me from the very first time I read about it. I thought the name, Salty Quill, was very cool and I was looking for a retreat in New England to appropriately begin my Thoreau book. Pam Loring, Co-Founder and Director, provides the perfect* atmosphere for us aspiring writers to immerse ourselves in our craft. She was leery, at first, to let me come, concerned I would want to kayak instead of write. I assured her this was about my writing, yet I did get out for a short paddle around the island a few of the days. I am so grateful she let me join!

I choose the Zora Neale Hurston room, described as the most serene in the house. A corner room with a queen bed, a small desk and views of the island interior, accessed via its own private entry from the side yard. Hurston was an American author, anthropologist and filmmaker, focusing her work on the experience of a black woman. Her most famous quote "Thoreau-ly" connected with me, "I have the nerve to walk my own way, however hard, in my search for reality, rather than climb upon the rattling wagon of wishful illusions."[8]

Each day is ours to shape. The weather is gloriously sunny and unseasonably warm with 60-degree temperatures. I chose a blend of being outside, with daily hikes around the island and kayaking, and spending quality time working on organizing the quotes and flow of this book. A bigger task than I realized.

Most days, I write at the little cherry wood desk in my room. One morning, just after sunrise, I take my notes and computer and hike to a little picnic table I spotted on a cliff just off the trail. The sea is in ebb tide, the tide turning around, glistening in the soft rays of the morning sun. I watch the lobster fishermen check their multicolored buoys. Work on the sea is beginning, and so I start, too, picking and choosing Thoreau quotes to reflect upon. I journal my own preliminary thoughts and it is my intention to establish the framework for this book during the week. I am happy to say, I accomplished this on McGee.

Each evening, we gather in the large living room around the hearthstone fireplace, plop ourselves into comfy overstuffed chairs and wicker rockers, and share our writing. Every evening two of us read our work out loud and receive feedback from the group. I am amazed at the incredible

119

*talent and the wide variety of genres – fiction, nonfiction, memoir and poetry. Just as am I surrounded by the dazzling Atlantic Ocean on this island, I am encircled in the brilliant creativity and comforting warmth of these women writers.*

*I interject here with wonderful news from home! My nephew Dan and his wife, Alaina, announce the birth of their daughter, Bianca Beverly Murawski. Mom, Dad and baby are all doing well. I can't wait to meet my new great-niece!*

*I become good friends with Joasha, our 87-year-old writer polishing up her novel, Rosa's Scarf, about a young couple struggling to stay together during World War II. Joasha is Polish and so am I, so we talk Polish to each other, much to everyone's "Oh brother, here they go again!" They had no idea what we were saying, and sometimes we didn't either!*

*Toward the end of the week, five of us - myself, Andrea, Fannie, Julie and Tara – the non-novelists of the group, gather in the warmth of the brightly lit sunroom for an intimate discussion of our work. It is the blossoming of a continued, supportive network of writers who have become friends. We Zoom once a month now, and had our first reunion in the Adirondack Mountains in New York in September, 2022. I am so grateful for this incredibly brilliant and fun-loving sisterhood of writers.*

*Our week of fabulous camaraderie comes to a close and it was sad to leave the sheltered space of this writing haven. It was everything I could imagine and so much more.*

View from the wraparound porch

# The Red Maple?

*"We had not gone far before I was startled by seeing what I thought was an Indian encampment, covered with a red flag, on the bank, and exclaimed, "Camp!" to my comrades. I was slow to discover that it was a red maple changed by the frost."*

-Henry David Thoreau, The Maine Woods, Chesuncook

Thoreau wrote this quote while he and his companions were paddling on the Penobscot River. They were on an exploratory trip of the area in the interior of Maine near Moosehead Lake. Their Penobscot Indian guide, Joe Polis, was out to hunt a moose.

Along the shoreline, Thoreau saw varied trees – white and black spruce, maple, black ash, aspen and elms. As he was observing these trees he proclaimed "Camp!" at the sight of what he thought was the red flag of an Indian camp, only to realize it was a red maple leaf.

They canoed further up Lobster Stream to Lobster Lake and then back on the Penobscot. In the evening, after they made their camp, they went on an unsuccessful shoreline hunt for moose.

Pencil sketch from photo of the decoy duck

121

## *Illusions*

In the shimmering silver light of a frosty October morning, I paddle near the reedy shoreline of the lake, content to kayak on the calm water, savoring the peacefulness of day's dawning. Soon, about 50 yards in the distance, I see a duck floating near the reeds. I continue to paddle closer to the duck, and it does not change its position. It does not move. It does not fly away. Strange I thought, but then again, it is duck hunting season so perhaps it knows to stay closely tucked into the safety of the reeds.

As I quietly edge closer, I realize why it has not moved. It is a decoy, floating motionless on the tranquil water. I smile and say, "Well the decoy really works!" This visual illusion distorted my perception and drew me in.

A decoy is defined as something that entices and lures. In the duck hunting world, a decoy lures live birds into an area by creating an illusion of safety.[9]

Suddenly, I see a skein of ducks fly overhead and hear shots ring out! Yikes, the hunters are near! Although I paddle in blaze orange clothing in the fall, I do not want to be part of the kill, so I quickly paddle to a safer area.

The red maple leaf and the decoy duck have me thinking about the illusions in my own life. How often, do I see one thing and think it is something else? How often do I create my own misrepresentations when my thoughts and feelings fail to align with my behavior?

To some degree we all do this. Is it for the allure of safety? Or protection? Or maybe sometimes we unintentionally create these misperceptions of who we really are?

I call these my blind spots. I have many of them, and one of my biggest ones is I believe I am always sincere with

122

my intentions. My intentions are always in the right place, I say. And yet there are times when other people don't see it that way. I feel they have misinterpreted my intention. Do they see something different in my motive? Is this an illusion I've created or are people seeing what they want to see in me? I often fail to realize that not everyone thinks as I do.

When I was a teenager, I had a long-sleeved, pumpkin-orange sweatshirt. On the front was a sketch of a dejected Charlie Brown, head down, standing on the pitcher's mound, glove hanging limp at his side. His team had lost another baseball game. The caption read, "How can we lose when we're so sincere?" I feel this way when my intentions are misunderstood. I wish I still had that sweatshirt!

If the decoy duck lures other birds in by creating an illusion of safety, I experienced an opposite perception on another kayaking morning. A few homes lined the shoreline paddling into Falls River Pond from the Connecticut River. Near one of the docks, the image of an alligator was peeking its head out of the water. Upon closer approach, it was a partially submerged log whose visible end took the shape of an alligator's head.

This decoy sent a warning signal to stay away. There is danger here in the pond! What a different impression from this discreetly concealed creature!

This time the illusion made me think of times when I sensed this same feeling from other people. Keep my distance. They do not look approachable. Was I accurate in my perception? Are there times when I send out a similar vibe creating an unwelcoming illusion?

Henry wrote in his journal, "The question is not what you look at, but what you see."[10] It can be confusing, but the answer lies in how well we know ourselves. When who we are inside matches how we show up in the outside world, the illusion disappears. If we turned ourselves inside out, we would be the same! No decoy!

When Henry saw the red maple leaf, he thought it was something else. When I saw the decoy duck and alligator log, I thought they were something else. This is a lesson in recognition. Blind spots are unconscious facets of ourselves. From time to time, we are unaware of the root cause of behaviors we exhibit.

To minimize these illusions in our lives, we must learn to create a deeper level of self-awareness, so we can bridge the gap between our inside and outside persons. Hello inner self, meet outer self. Let's show our true selves together! Our false appearances last for a short time, before they are exposed for their misleading image.

Some of us are further along on this path of mindfulness than others. Self-aware people are happier, have better relationships, are clear about their values and recognize the effect they have on others. They are better decision makers and communicate with clarity and intention.[11] Sounds like a wonderful place, but how do we get there?

*************

Here are a few suggestions from Henry:
- Do what you love.
- Do not entertain doubts if they are not agreeable to you.
- As for health, consider yourself well.
- Do not engage to find things as you think they are.
- Do what nobody else can do for you.
- Omit to do anything else.
- Let nothing come between you and the light.[12]

# Spires

*"Strange that so few ever come to the woods
to see how the pine lives and grows and spires,
lifting its evergreen arms to the light, - to see its
perfect success; but most are content to behold
it in the shape of many broad boards brought
to market, and deem that its true success!"*

-Henry David Thoreau, The Maine Woods, Chesuncook

During the afternoon, Thoreau's party killed a moose while paddling on Pine Stream to Chesuncook Lake. Thoreau had not come to the woods for this purpose. He wrote, "The afternoon's tragedy, and my share in it, as it affected the innocence, destroyed the pleasure of my adventure." He compared this experience to shooting a neighbor's horse, only this was God's own horse.[13]

Thoreau was melancholy, sitting alone by his campfire, while his companions went canoeing to hunt down another moose. He purposely stayed back writing, "Nature looked sternly upon me on account of the murder of the moose."[14] He was dejected.

He sullenly muses how an elephant is slain for its ivory, and the pine tree cut down for lumber. He watches the pine spires "waving and reflecting the light at a distance high over all the rest of the forest." He writes, "It is not their bones or hide or tallow that I love most. It is the living spirit of the tree..."[15] Thoreau was relieved when the hunters returned emptyhanded.

Pencil sketch from photo of towering spires

127

# *Our Pillars of Life*

The pencil sketch is from a photo of the spires I see on my frequent paddles up and down the slowly meandering waters of White Sand Creek. The creek is an offshoot of the Manitowish River, and the tops of these green vertical towers sway in the soft morning breeze, just as Henry had seen from his seat by the campfire.

As I glance up at these towering spires, they remind me of my pillars of life. I envision these spires as strong backbones to the forest, just as my pillars bring me strength. They remind me to grow, to stretch myself.

My four pillars are: EMOTIONAL, SPIRITUAL, FINANCIAL and PHYSICAL. Others may categorize things differently, but for me these four encompass a complete life. Every year, I set an intention to reevaluate these four areas monthly. Do I do it? Not consistently!

Some items have been on my list for years, and some eventually come off the list. Those I eliminate may have benefited me in the past, but, in time I find they no longer serve me. In any event, the steadfast, towering presence of these spires keeps my intentions in view.

In some years, the focus is more on one pillar than the others. Sometimes, I tend to them equally. But over time I have learned not to get frustrated if they are not all expanding in the same way. It is more important for them to flow in harmony, than to be in exact balance.

Each year, however, I do review them and assess what I have done in each area to enhance the next evolution of my life. Or what I have not done – those go on next year's list!

As my little red kayak and I maneuver the twists and turns of the creek, I look upward at the tips of these pines and I think about each of these spires of my life.

In my EMOTIONAL pillar, I put questions like: How do I want to feel today? How do I express my feelings in the best way? And I run many things through my "is this healthy for me?" filter.

My SPIRITUAL pillar includes these intentions: To approach each day with tenderness, kindness and gratitude. To keep my spirit fully at peace in my mind and heart.

In my FINANCIAL pillar, I take tender care of ALL my resources. How do I successfully manage my finances to provide for myself? How can I be unboundedly generous? How can I direct my resources and energy to fill a need?

Finally, my PHYSICAL pillar contains actions to keep myself as healthy as possible. My Grandmother Mary, who lived to 101, said, "If you have your health, you have everything." She was absolutely right.

Those are the broad brush strokes of my pillars and each year, within them I include specific stepping stones. Small footbridges on my winding pathway of personal growth. Like the twists and turns of the bends of a river.

As my view gazes up at the sun kissed spires standing like sentinels at water's edge, I am reminded of their interconnectedness. And their precariousness. Should one of these ascending steeples topple or become weakened the others are negatively impacted.

So too, with our pillars. If one is out of balance, if one falters or is temporarily fractured, the others suffer as well. They share a fragile, cohesive bond. To periodically

129

reinforce them, and rebuild if necessary, keeps our structure strong for the long duration of our lives.

Your pillars might be different, but the most important thing is that we *have* pillars. We need a framework for important areas of our lives to tend to regularly.

As I paddle back into the Manitowish River from the creek, I turn left with the current. The expanse of the river looms large after paddling in the intimate creek. I think I just kayaked onto the Mississippi River!

After Henry and his companions left the smaller Pine Stream and canoed into the vastness of Chesuncook Lake, he wrote, "...it is not often that the stream of our life opens into such expansions..."[16]

Our pillars may be narrow and towering, but they lead us to expansion and new heights, joyfully spiraling upward with the unsuppressed rhythms of our lives.

Just as the spires grace the edges of the creek, so too, our pillars of life line our shoreline, guiding us, directing us and helping us stay on course.

*************

*What are the pillars of your life?*

*How can you create a simple plan to focus on them regularly?*

*How do you allow them to flow with the ever-changing currents of your life?*

# Thoreau

131

## Summiting Mt. Kineo
### Moosehead Lake, Rockwood, Maine
### Elevation 1,789 ft.
### June 8, 2022

July 20-August 8, 1857 - Thoreau with Concord attorney, Edward Hoar and Penobscot Indian guide, Joe Polis, took his last Maine trip which involved an overnight stay at Kineo. Sometime during this period after dinner one evening, they began their climb to the summit.

*As I prepare for my ascent, I write this note to carry, connecting Henry and me more deeply on this climb:*

Dear Henry,
Although I will not be overnight on this summit, today is my birthday and I can't think of a greater gift to me than to be hiking this mountain which you summited.

Your quote, "...having no particular home, but equally at home everywhere,"[17] is in my thoughts today.

June 8, 2022 - I hope to summit Mt. Kineo in honor of you on my 67th birthday. What a gift, and as I climb today, I hope to embrace the gift of your quote above, to be "at home" wherever I am. Climbing Kineo, I will ponder that thought as a gift to myself and what I can offer to others, being mindful of how I show up in the world...every single day.

"To elevate myself as I begin my new year, is my birthday gift to myself. Sto lat!"
- *Mary Anne Smrz*

*Sharp winds, a light drizzle and dense fog greet us this morning. Ominous charcoal black and steel gray clouds encircle the mountain, cloaking the peak with an uninviting veil. A mysterious, inclement summit hike awaits.*

*Mt. Kineo sits on Mt. Kineo State Park peninsula on Moosehead Lake. The largest freshwater lake contained in one state east of the Mississippi River, Moosehead is 40 miles*

133

*long and ten miles wide, with 80 islands. The brochure touts pictures of stunning lake views, wide open vistas and glorious mountain and lake scenery that can be seen for miles. Uh, not so much today.*

*Getting to Mt. Kineo, with no road access, requires catching a ferry at the Rockwood Boat Landing for a ten-minute ride across the lake to the peninsula. Dee and I catch the 9 a.m. ferry to begin our Kineo adventure.*

*We speak to the ferry driver about the trail we are planning to hike, but due to the rain the previous night, he suggests we hike up and down Bridle Trail, instead of the steeper Indian Trail. Being unfamiliar with the trails, we take his suggestion and were glad we did.*

*After a half mile circling the bottom of the mountain, we begin our ascent. The trail is lush with fluorescent green ferns and early June wildflowers shimmering in the morning mist. The heavier rain subsides and the wind sends down soft droplets of water from the deep, verdant green pines.*

*We watch our footing on the slippery rocks and oversized tree roots as we head up, breathing in the freshness that the rain has brought to this wooded climb. I love the smell of the pines after a rainfall.*

*At 10:50 a.m. we reach the summit, which on Mt. Kineo looks no different than the woods we have just hiked through. To really see the summit view, a five-story fire tower climb is a must. The shrouded gray, misty surroundings provide no stunning views as stated in the brochure, but we climb anyway. It is part of today's experience and although we see nothing but fog, we look down on the spires of the pine trees, sparkling with drizzly rain drops, and smile. This is all we see, standing in the cloudbank on the tower. Yet it mirrors the experience Henry had at the summit as he wrote in* The Maine Woods, *"Looking southward, the heavens were completely overcast, the mountains capped with clouds, and the lake generally wore a dark and stormy appearance..."*[18]

134

*We are glad to have climbed the fire tower and begin our gradual descent. Heading down, I ponder his quote about being equally at home wherever you are. It takes a great deal of inner reserve to feel that way, and on this, my birthday, I commit to being conscious of that concept in my next 365.*

*I concentrate also on the word "sauntering" Henry used many times in his writings as I slowly come down the mountain. If I had gone faster, I would have missed the evidence of moose on Kineo! I compare our soggy saunter to his experience here. He wrote, "If I wished to see a mountain or other scenery under the most favorable auspices, I would go to it in foul weather, so as to be there when it cleared up; we are then in the most suitable mood, and nature is more fresh and inspiring. There is no serenity so fair as that which is just established in a tearful eye."[19]*

*The weather starts to clear as we walk across the bog boards on the lower portion of Kineo, and as we circle the exterior, two common loons accompany us in the water around the lakeshore trail. They are bobbing up and down as they ride the small swells driven by the continuing blustery wind.*

*We stop at the Mt. Kineo Golf Course – yes, you read that right, there is a golf course on the peninsula – for a bathroom break before boarding the 12:45 p.m. shuttle to Rockwood.*

*This Mt. Kineo peninsula has an interesting history. By 1855, two years before Henry's ascent, there was a resort house with a bowling alley. In 1884, a new resort was built after a fire at the old one, complete with a bowling alley, library, golf course, tennis courts, a baseball diamond, croquet lawns and a horseback riding area. The complex held two concerts daily and the dining room seated over 400 people. Mt. Kineo was known as a vacation resort for the rich and influential. Not the kind of nature destination Henry would have envisioned.*

*Today, all that remains is a scenic nine-hole golf course and several privately owned cottages. Quite a stark contrast from*

135

Kineo's wooded trails and the cliffs that are home to the peregrine falcons.

We board our ferry back to Rockwood, content with the unique hiking and summiting experience, feeling the satisfaction of hiking out of our comfort zone on this rainy day. Sometimes, the gifts we least expect are what we need. Nature knows. Happy Birthday!

Thoreau summited on July 24, 1857, age 40, with Ebenezer Hoar.

*Fire Tower at the summit of Mt. Kineo*
*Pencil sketch from photo by Dee Beckmann*

# Rogue Waves

*"Looking off from a lee shore, the surface
may appear to be very little agitated, almost
smooth, a mile distant, or if you see a few white
crests they appear nearly level with the rest
of the lake; but when you get out so far, you
may find quite a sea running, and erelong, before
you think of it, a wave will gently creep up the
side of the canoe and fill your lap..."*

-Henry David Thoreau, *The Maine Woods,
The Allegash and East Branch*

Thoreau made this observation as he, his companion
and the Indian guide, Joe Polis, were crossing a broad
bay on Moosehead Lake, opposite the mouth of the
Moose River. They were approaching the narrow strait at
Mount Kineo.

As previously described, Moosehead Lake stretches 40
miles long and ten miles wide, and has over 80 islands.
It is the largest mountain lake in the eastern United
States and the slightest blustery wind can stir up "rogue
waves." Thoreau and company found rough waters
through this passage. Later that day they landed,
prepared camp and summited Mount Kineo.

FLOAT PLAN

Paddlin'

## Expect the Unexpected

Rogue waves are defined as unusually large and unpredictable surface waves that seem to appear out of nowhere and can be extremely dangerous. Henry's quote reminded me of not only the disastrous impacts of large rogue waves, but also of the consequences of smaller "not so rogue" waves.

Rogue waves are considered rare occurrences. About one in every 10,000 waves is a rogue wave, the largest of which was recorded on January 1, 1995, in the North Sea with a maximum wave height of 84 feet.[20]

Globally, we have all experienced the unsettling and unpredictable effects of "rogue waves." The worldwide effects of the Covid-19 pandemic, devastating and costly climate events, mass shootings and ongoing wars, to name a few of the negative undertows. A huge rogue wave is swamping us.

Yet riding high on the crest of these breakers are healthy medical breakthroughs, forward thinking technological advances, people bonding together in times of crisis and our younger generations making positive contributions to our world. Swells of a promising future.

How well we navigate the choppiness of our existence today is critical to how we function as a society in the future. This massive transition gives reason to pause, to carefully choose how we collectively move forward.

We look in the rearview mirror at the events that have shaped us, both good and bad and know we can't go back. Henry wrote in *Walden*, "Don't destroy your peace of mind by looking back, worrying about the past."[21] We can only take our lessons from the past to help us move forward.

Over the years, kayaking has given me many gifts. Today's paddle is no exception, allowing time to pause on the lake to reflect on, and look out for, rogue waves!

Allowing ourselves the power of the pause helps us to discern our own individual next steps. When we quiet down, as kayaking has consistently helped me do, we get to a place inside where our answers lie. Deep beneath the surface of our busyness and hectic pace, there is a calm spot. A tranquil spot. A silent spot. The answers for each of us lie in this contemplative container of silence.

This morning on the lake, I watch nature begin to transform herself from a cold, long winter to a brighter, warmer spring. She shows us the way, to s-l-o-w-l-y move from one phase of life to the next. Watching the flow of this transition allows my thoughts to connect. Fragmented sound bites cease their disruptiveness.

How do we now individually move to a better season of our lives? Quieting down starts us on the path. But I think we also need a plan.

In kayaking, there is a document called a Float Plan. Kayakers are asked to complete it before going on the water. You fill in the date, anticipated length of your excursion, who you are paddling with or solo, your anticipated route, color of your boat and Personal Flotation Device (PFD), cell phone number and any other pertinent information.

Should unexpected "rogue waves" swamp you, someone on shore knows your plan and can provide rescue. It can mean the difference between a minor inconvenience and a full blown emergency.

A Float Plan not only serves to let others know our intentions, but also helps us to make our choices, both for kayaking and in life. When do we start? How far do we go? In what direction? Do we go solo or take others?

Going forward, we need both a collective and an individual Float Plan. It gives us a way to connect to each other, to let each other know how we intend to contribute to becoming part of the solution to a happier, more peaceful world. We can all stay afloat on these rogue and "not so rogue" waves of our lives, and safely navigate both calm and turbulent waters.

A Float Plan allows us to prepare for a good outcome. What might initially appear to be a terrible situation may ultimately prove beneficial. By considering next steps before reacting to the unexpected, we tap the power of the pause. Thoughtful response enables us to ride the waves, rogue or not, to the shores of acceptance.

And let's remember to trust that we will be okay. We have been through all heights of rogue waves in our lives and have come through. With our pause, our Float Plan and our ability to respond mindfully, we can minimize the debilitating effects of the negative waves and maximize the positive outflow.

*************

*How have you handled your rogue or "not so rogue" waves in the past and how has that served you?*

*Where is your quiet place to pause?*

*What would you include on your life's Float Plan?*

# The Call of the Loon

*"In the middle of the night, as indeed each time that we lay on the shore of a lake, we heard the voice of the loon, loud and distinct, from far over the lake. It is a very wild sound, quite in keeping with the place and the circumstances of the traveler, and very unlike the voice of a bird. I could lie awake for hours listening to it, it is so thrilling."*

-Henry David Thoreau, The Maine Woods,
The Allegash and East Branch

On his third and last excursion to the Maine woods in July of 1857, age 40, Thoreau was accompanied by one companion and the Indian guide, Joe Polis. They canoed across Moosehead Lake and into this region of the East Branch of the Penobscot River to Chamberlain Lake.

Their wet clothes clung heavily, muddy from the day's trek, and they walked waist deep in the lake to wash them. They were happy to find this dry, shoreline respite.

All day and into the evening, they swatted mosquitoes, black flies and no-see-ems. The campfire smoke kept these "insect foes," as Thoreau called them, at bay. Nightfall found them sleeping under the stars on a thin bed of grass covering the pebbly shore.

During this still night, the loon's wail broke the silence.

Pencil sketch from photo of the loon

# *Soul Sound*

There are sensory wonders of nature that stir my soul.

The gentle hoot of an owl stirs my soul. I hear the distinctive calls at night – the unmistakable *"who cooks for you?"* of the Barred Owl or the soft *"hoo-hoo-hoo-hoo"* of the Great Horned Owl. No matter the depth of my slumber, their soulful whispers awaken me. I smile.

The smell of a salt marsh stirs my soul. Although it is referred to as a "rotten egg" aroma, I happen to love it. When I close my eyes at water's edge and inhale, I feel something ancient, something deeply primeval. I smile.

But there is nothing like the haunting call of the loon to stir my soul. When I am paddling on the lake or asleep in the middle of the night, the distant wail of mated loons communicating, or the male's territorial yodel, sends tingles up and down my spine. Their calls reach into the deep marrow of my soul. I smile.

I paddle one of the smaller lakes in the northwoods today. In 2021, John Bates, a respected well-known local nature writer published a book called, *Wisconsin's Wild Lakes*. His criteria included lakes under a certain size, no homes on the lake and no large watercraft allowed. Small intimate lakes. Serene. More primitive. My friends and I try to paddle one of these every week. We call them our "Bates Lakes." I feel this setting is perfect for some soul-searching. To answer these deeper questions:

What is my soul? Where is my soul? How do I know when I am living in alignment with my soul?

I Google "what is the soul?" Google knows all the answers, right? A myriad of responses come up. The soul is our source of intuition. The soul is the energy of our core, our true nature. The soul is our connection to the divine and our moral compass providing direction. The soul is our inner knowing and its existence is eternal. We pray for the souls of our departed loved ones.

If the soul is all of that, and I believe it is and more, how do we live our lives in alignment with it? How do we know when we are deeply connected to our soul? Henry asked this question, "With all your science can you tell how it is, and whence it is, that light comes into the soul?"[22]

Today I paddle Frog Lake, 42 acres of land-locked water nestled in the Frog Lake Natural Preserve. One of Bates' Lakes. I portage in, dragging my little red vessel over a narrow path of moist pine needles about 1/8 mile to the put in, which is a very small inconspicuous spot on the shore. The afternoon is breezy and the many lily pads along the shore encroach toward the middle of the lake, making it seem even smaller than its tiny 42 acres.

I am thinking of my friend, Dr. Cathy Taphorn, the holistic veterinarian who took care of my yellow lab, Bayfield. In today's mail, I receive a note from her and it made me smile seeing her name on the envelope. In her note, thanking me for our friendship over the years, she wrote, "By the time you receive this, I will have passed." Stunned and shaken, I sit down, trembling. Her beautiful 55-year-old life cut short by the ravages of ALS, I read. Apparently she instructed her husband, Scott, to mail her notes after she died. She was a peaceful, gentle person so this tender gesture was no surprise. Her obituary requested no monetary contributions, simply asking we be kind to one another. I prayed for her. She lived her life aligned with her soul.

As I paddle around Frog Lake, I have faith that every element of nature has a soul. Henry believed there was a soul-force connecting all creatures, human and non-human. Nature is the single unifying place. He wrote, "Our life revolves unceasingly, but the centre is ever the same, and the wise will regard only the seasons of the soul."[23]

When we look at our lives, and feel "something is missing" or we are searching for "something more," or we sense an unexplainable emptiness, that is when we have lost connection to our soul. I believe everyone is inherently good, and when people are cruel, angry, and divisive, focused on negative and ego-driven outcomes, they have lost connection to their soul. When people are overly focused on material wealth and things of this world, they have lost connection to their soul.

There are many ways to reconnect to our soul. Focus on what is truly important. Spend solitude time in nature. Search for something deeply meaningful and go for it. Dare to "walk to the beat of a different drummer," as Henry would say. This is an uncomfortable path because most people prefer complacency and mediocrity, or in Henry's words, "quiet desperation."[24]

The people who make a difference in life, the people whose universal messages stand the test of time, are the ones who walk the path of their soul. They pave the way for us to do the same. Nature is the universal place where the soul of all life remains constant. She holds the essential life force, the light of the soul.

The owl, the salt marsh, the loon. They know.

*************

*What elements in nature call to the depths of your soul?*

*How can you spend time with nature every day to consistently connect to your soul?*

*How can you illuminate the inner room of your soul and feel fully alive?*

146

# Canoeing Prong Pond
## Greenville, Maine
## June 7, 2022

For many years I wanted to see and experience Moosehead Lake near Greenville, Maine. Nestled in the majestic mountain ranges, it is the largest lake in Maine. At 40 miles long and ten miles wide, it is no small body of water. The lake has 80 islands, Sugar and Deer Islands being the largest. Going to Moosehead as part of my Thoreau journey is perfect, as he canoed here on his visits to Maine. He referred to Moosehead "like a gleaming silver platter at the end of the table."[25] Serve it up, I say!

The day after our amazing summit of Mt. Katahdin, Dee and I drive almost 60 miles west, further into the interior of Maine, to Greenville. Our intention is to paddle on Moosehead Lake like Thoreau, and my excitement is building with each passing mile. The sunny, 70-degree day seems to present perfect conditions, but a blustery wind is brewing and getting stronger as we approach. We thought perhaps our kayak excursion might not materialize.

We arrive at Northwoods Outfitters in Greenville and talk to Pat, an expert on the local waters who confirms our paddling concerns. She indicates the wind will be increasing all day presenting undesirable and unsafe kayaking on Moosehead.

She presents an alternative paddling option and we agree. Six miles north of Greenville on the southeast side of Moosehead Lake, lies beautiful Prong Pond. Northwoods Outfitters keeps rental canoes at the pond and she gives us the key to the padlock and hands us our canoe paddles. With the wind stirring Moosehead to a frothy cocktail, this segue to Prong Pond seems ideal.

I must admit I was disappointed not to paddle on Moosehead Lake like Thoreau. Another time. But going to Prong Pond is serendipitous. I have a book called Quiet Waters that

149

features smaller lakes and waters to paddle in Maine. Before we left, I made a copy of the information about Prong Pond, knowing it was near Moosehead and "just in case" we could paddle there, I wanted to be prepared. No coincidences.

Prong Pond flows into Beaver Creek and then Beaver Cove, which ultimately empties into Moosehead Lake. So I feel as though I am paddling a unique extension of Moosehead Lake. Good enough for me.

It has been a very long time since I have been in a canoe, the kayak being my preferred mode of water transportation for the last 27 years. But with padlock key and canoe paddles in hand, we drive to Prong Pond.

It is the perfect gem of a spot to paddle on this windy day, and with our snackage for lunch and plenty of water, we canoe onto its fairly calm waters on the north side of the pond. From our vantage point just off the launch area, we could see Prong Pond Mountain. A beautiful vista in the distance providing a panoramic feeling to our paddle.

Prong Pond has narrow arms extending to the east and west, thus I assume, the name "Prong." This body of water is 427 acres with a perimeter of nine miles providing exploration of cozy coves and intriguing inlets. We melted into these "nooks and crannies®" like butter on a Thomas® English muffin.

We avoid the east arm due to its shallow, boggy nature and instead canoe around some of the little islands and continue to navigate and investigate the rocky shoreline. We take a lunch break near the south end of the pond and feel the wind increasing in strength. Our canoe is moving sideways now as we take the last bites of our peanut butter sandwiches and contemplate heading back to the launch.

And then we hear it so close to us that our heads snap simultaneously in the same direction. The haunting, magical wail of the loon. About 50 yards off the right side of our canoe, there she is. I don't know why I always refer to loons as "she." She is content to bob on the pond's surface as she searches for food underneath. We sit in silence and watch her, mesmerized by her beauty and her haunting call.

Hearing and watching a loon is a spiritual experience for me. This sacred encounter tethers me to the edge of eternity. Being with her only added to the deeper connection I feel all day to the wildness of Maine.

Thoreau wrote in his essay "Walking," "In Wildness is the preservation of the World."[26] Canoeing "Thoreau-like" today enhances my craving for wildness. Although our Hunter green canoe was not made of birch bark like the days of old, I embrace the sensation of an early explorer, seeking new paths where no one has gone before. The richness of this experience is exhilarating.

The blustery winds continue, so after our two-hour excursion, we paddle back to the launch. The day provides an unexpected gift of canoeing on Prong Pond, instead of kayaking on Moosehead Lake. A wilderness connection to Thoreau I never expected or planned.

That evening, sitting on the bench on our balcony, I hear the loon yodeling in the distance on Moosehead Lake. The timeless, enduring voice of the eternal, of the soul. A fitting close to the day. I smile and I am grateful.

Pencil sketch from photo on Prong Pond, Prong Mountain in view

151

# Thoreau

## *Cape Cod*
### Originally Published Posthumously in 1865

After Thoreau's death in 1862, his sister, Sophia and his traveling companion, Ellery Channing, organized and edited his manuscript and published *Cape Cod* three years later.

Thoreau first visited the Cape in October, 1849 at age 32, with his hiking companion and friend, Ellery Channing. He returned three times, alone in June of 1850, with Ellery Channing again in July, 1855, and alone in June, 1857. He hiked its entire length from Sandwich to Provincetown and stopped at places in between. He also sauntered across the Cape, from the Atlantic Ocean shore to Cape Cod Bay on the other side.

In the introduction of my 1987 edition of *Cape Cod*, Paul Theroux, writes, "To him, (Thoreau) Cape Cod was not a territory to be explored; it was a vantage point." Thoreau's final thoughts on the Cape were, "A man may stand there and put all America behind him."[1]

From this vantage point on shore I write my essays.

Shoreline of Cape Cod

153

# Channeled Whelk

*"We eagerly filled our pockets with the smooth round
pebbles which in some places, even here, were thinly
sprinkled over the sand, together with flat circular shells;
but, as we had read, when they were dry they had lost
their beauty, and at each sitting we emptied our pockets
again of the least remarkable, until our collection
was well culled."*

-Henry David Thoreau, Cape Cod, The Beach Again

We've all done this, right? Walked a beach filled with
glistening sea shells tumbled onto the shore by the surf
and lined our bulging pockets with low-tide treasures.

Thoreau wrote this quote after they left their visit with
the Wellfleet Oysterman and scaled the banks on the
south part of Truro. Henry was mesmerized by all of the
objects on the beach – clam shells and barnacles, faded
washed up buoys with parts of the line intact, bones
from fish and maybe human remains?, boards and
remnants of shipwrecks.

I doubt I ever walked his same paths here. The people at
Cape Cod National Seashore tell me much of his path is
now covered by the sea. But I have explored many of
Thoreau's places on Cape Cod and today, I share with
you the story of my find, the Channeled Whelk.

## *Cycle of Life*

I have a huge, clear vase filled with colorful treasures of the sea I have collected over the years.

My newly found channeled whelk, however, sits alone on my desk, front and center as I write, beautifully spiraling and to me, perfect in shape. Here is her story.

I am on Cape Cod visiting my dear friend and author, Joan Anderson, whose husband, Robin, recently passed away. I am with her for a time, processing and sharing our grief, and I take a much needed beach walk.

A crystal clear morning welcomes me as I plant my feet on the soggy sand of the beach. A soft ocean breeze greets me and I revel in the smell of the salty air. A seagull squawks overhead and another runs frantically along the shore. I am surrounded by the life of the sea.

I think about Robin, a wonderful friend to me, and about how life and death are continuing cycles. There is no better place than the ocean to ponder these thoughts, the sea full of cycles every day. I walk at low tide now where everything is exposed, and as I amble along, a bright green flicker of color catches my eye. Partially exposed in the sand lies the most beautiful, complete channeled whelk. The green hue I see on the shell, still wet from the surf, glistens in the sun.

What a perfect shell to find for this moment. At one time, a sea snail inhabited this spiral shape, but now the home is vacant. No more life within the shell. It has left its protection. Just like Robin, leaving his earthly shelter.

Throughout my life I have gone in and out of protection. There are times I feel the need to protect myself and my heart, and other times I need to open wide. "Smrzy, you are the most vulnerable person I know," Robin would tell

156

me. He showered me with this deep and tender compliment and my heart knows what a daunting challenge it is to remain vulnerable at all times. But I hear his words echoing across the sparkling surface of the sea. He is right. I run my salty fingers up and down the perfect contour of the channeled whelk. Each sandy, windswept furrow a different emotion perhaps, spiraling in harmony? Yes. There is a symmetry to this shell as there is an equilibrium to life. I must keep the shoreline of my heart open to all the waves of emotion. In all the cycles of life.

In nature, spirals represent the rhythm of life. Spiritually, "spirals represent our journey through life, death and rebirth... and the interconnectedness of all life. We are all part of the same ebb and flow."[2]

This description leads my thoughts to infinite expansion as part of our cycle of life. I like to keep expanding and growing, and the intricate beauty of the channeled whelk reminds me to grow and adapt and embrace the ever-evolving twists and turns life sends my way.

I saunter away from the water to the higher dunes of the beach, taking a closer look at the seaweed green clumps of dune grass. I watch intently as one of its long narrow leaves gently spins around in the breeze, its tip leaning down, forming a perfectly complete circle in the sand. The circle of life. Nature is amazing in her coastal lessons on the wholeness of life.

These dune grasses also symbolize infinite expansion, spreading their fragile ecosystem on the sandy surface anchored by a strong root system below. Henry, ever the botanist, once tried to uproot a cluster of this defiant beach grass, only to discover its depth and strength held firm. There is power in their fragility.

157

At Robin's memorial service, we sang the song "Balm of Gilead." The lyrics begin, "There is a balm in Gilead to make the wounded whole..."[3] At the time, I did not know there are trees called Balm of Gilead. When Henry was on Cape Cod, he saw them near Provincetown.[4] They grow well in moist sandy soil near water[5] so of course he would have seen this tree. My current of thought flows to the healing properties of this tree, often used for herbal medicines, making the wounded whole. The intangible connection to Robin and the continuity of life continues to grace my seaside sojourn.

The shoreline is an impermanent terrain between distinct landscapes, the sea and the land. As Joan says, "I am as unfinished as the shoreline along the beach, meant to transcend myself again and again."

Robin has transcended, yet his spirit lives on in each of us. The channeled whelk and dune grass teach me lessons today of infinite expansion and continuity of life. The Balm of Gilead reminds me that healing is essential to living a full life.

In his journal, Henry wrote, "Every part of nature teaches that the passing away of one life is the making room for another."[6]

And the cycle of life continues.

*************

*Can you remember a time you were reminded of the circle of life?*

*How deeply did that time affect you? Did it cause you to make any changes in your life?*

*What one element of nature reminds you that the passing away of one life makes room for another?*

# Give Me Shelter

*"But I wished to see that seashore where man's works are wrecks; to put up at the true Atlantic House, where the ocean is land-lord as well as sea-lord, and comes ashore without a wharf for the landing;..."*

-Henry David Thoreau, Cape Cod, The Beach

Thoreau is hiking from Nauset Beach to Race Point in Provincetown when he wrote this quote. The hallmarks of Nauset Beach are long stretches of sandy beach and high dune banks. A place where pounding surf and rolling waves get inside you. He writes you can see for miles down the coast and "There I had got the Cape under me, as much as if I were riding it bare-backed." He fell in love with its wildness, writing, "But there I found it all out of doors, huge and real, Cape Cod!"[7]

Frequent shipwrecks occurred along this stretch of wildness. The "Trustees of the Humane Society have erected huts called Charity or Humane Houses..."[8] and published *The Shipwrecked Seaman's Manual* indicating shoreline havens of shelter for shipwrecked seamen.

Pencil sketch from photo of a seaside hut on Cape Cod

161

## *Protection*

I took this essay off my list, but the pencil sketch of the picture of the small hut near Chatham on Cape Cod called me to write. It is not one of the "Charity Huts" Henry referred to, but it sure looks like a sweet place to find shelter if needed.

Genius Loci.

This Latin term that originated in Roman mythology is defined as "the protective spirit of a place."[9] Every place has a spirit about it, an energy. Today, holistic architects create environments of continuity based on the authenticity of a location, blending the tangible, physical elements with its intangible, spiritual vitality. They protect the unique and distinguishing aspects of a place. And they call it Genius Loci.[10]

As I walk the shores of Cape Cod today, I ponder what it is to provide a "protective spirit." The brave, shipwrecked seafaring sailors who washed up on shore, were seeking shelter. The survival huts along the Cape provided these men with one of life's basic needs, shelter, for protection and safety. A place to stay alive against the odds.

As I begin to think about the many ways we protect ourselves, I realize every aspect of our lives is impacted. Here is a small sampling:
- In numerous ways, we protect our children and loved ones;
- We use medicine of all types to ensure good health;
- We have insurance to safeguard our possessions and ourselves;
- We have clothing to protect us from the elements and safety equipment to shield us from danger;
- We have security to protect our property, our identity, and firewalls to defend our computers;

162

- We have laws to guard us against a menagerie of actual and perceived dangers.

The list goes on and on. We are obsessed with protecting the physical, tangible ingredients of our lives. One part of Genius Loci.

As I tenderly stroll along the fragile ecosystem of the Cape, I marvel at the way nature protects herself. Let's look at a few seaside examples:
- Sea turtles have protective shells to ward off predators;
- Many fish swim in schools to evade danger;
- Crabs often hide in seaweed for shelter and hermit crabs burrow in the sand;
- Seals, sea lions, sea otters and even gray whales take cover in sea kelp for protection.[11]

So what about our other part of Genius Loci, the intangible, spiritual element? How do we protect her?

Our spirits need to heal. We need a time out from all our justifiable distractions. We crave a slower pace to stitch ourselves back together. Where do we turn? To nature. The harbinger of all the healing balm we will ever need. Walks in the woods, strolling through a park, kayaking on a tranquil lake, sitting by a seashore, and more provide us much needed shelter for our spirits from the fury of our fast paced life. Nature is our sanctuary. Our Genius Loci.

Recent books, such as *The Nature Fix: Why Nature Makes us Happier, Healthier, and More Creative* by Florence Williams, and *Braiding Sweetgrass* by Robin Wall Kimmerer illustrate the healing, restorative and protective benefits of time spent in the natural world. Ecotherapy, often referred to as Nature Therapy, is emerging as a prescription for inner healing.

163

Nature provides a safe haven to tend to us and in turn, we must care for her. We are feeling the effects of neglecting natures' needs by our destructive actions in the name of progress. When we protect her forests, waterways and atmosphere, we shield ourselves from the devastating effects of viruses, floods and drought. When "unprecedented" and "catastrophic" become casual, commonplace words, it is time to build protective havens for nature to thrive instead of merely survive. She is our global safe harbor. She is the healing bridge that connects us all.

In October of 2019, the UN Environment Programme (UNEP) put out this statement, "When we protect nature, nature protects us." There is reciprocity in those words.

Their statement would resonate with Henry, who found all his answers in nature, his Genius Loci.

*************

*Where do you go to find protection and shelter?*

*Is it a place, time with other people, time alone?*

*How often can you go to your survival hut?*

*What one thing can you do today to protect nature?*

165

# Shipwrecked

*"You would sometimes see an old oar used for a rail."*

-Henry David Thoreau, Cape Cod, Across the Cape

As best as I can tell, Thoreau has now walked to Truro and here on these amber waves of windswept sand, he writes this quote. Meandering up and down the uneven shoreline, he sees remnants of shipwrecks.

Talking with the locals, he learns many windmills, parts of bridges and rails for fencing were built with shipwrecked wood. Among other things, a lighthouse keeper told him he found enough material from an old mast to make 3,000 shingles for his barn.

His musings continue, "To the fisherman, the Cape itself is a sort of store-ship laden with supplies..."[12]

Driftwood hut
Photo by Dee Beckmann

## *Preservation*

The photo of the seaside shelter on the previous page was taken at Hammonasset Beach on the shore of Long Island Sound in Madison, Connecticut. A careful selection of driftwood is repurposed for the building of this one-person wooden hut. I cherish my fond memories of walking this beach with Dee's family – Scott, Fei, Bruce, Chelsea, Lila and their doxies, Indie and Ranger.

The farmers and fisherman on the Cape are keenly aware of the importance of the preservation of both the natural and man-made gifts from the ocean. These watchmen of the sea are the safe-keepers of these windswept and waterlogged riches seeking a new home, a new purpose.

As I walk along the Cape Cod beach today, I gaze out onto the vastness of the cool aqua ocean and I wonder what distant remnants are working their way towards shore to be repurposed as cherished lasting treasures.

I think about our lives today. We live in a throwaway society, discarding items that are washed up. When our refrigerator stops, we don't repair it. We get a new one. Family heirlooms are no longer treasured for their sentimental value. We are barely out of the shadow of a broken relationship when we start our search for another. Everything goes overboard!

I am all about letting go of what or who no longer serves me. Life is too short to spin about in an eddy of unhealthy stuff and people. But it is the *way* we discard things and people that has become so casual. The parts of our lives that were so important yesterday, become instantly insignificant today. We discard what has been sacred to us as quickly as we toss out a candy wrapper.

What has happened to us? I ponder this question on my beach walk. What do we preserve and why?

168

We preserve our photos for the memories they invoke after time has passed. We preserve food by freezing and canning to enjoy at a later date. We preserve natural environments to protect them from future development.

But what about some of our unveiled truths, our deeper held values we would like to preserve? Let me share an interesting concept that has resurfaced for me as I look out across the cobalt blue surface at the infinite horizon.

It is the notion of an ethical will. A number of years ago I read an interesting book titled, *Ethical Wills: Putting Your Values on Paper* by Barry K. Baines, M.D. The premise of writing an ethical will is outlined in his detailed overview. "Those who want to be remembered authentically and for their gifts of heart, mind, and spirit take satisfaction in knowing what they hold most valued is 'on the record,' not to be lost or forgotten."[13]

He provides guided exercises and contemplation prompts for writing down our values, beliefs, thoughts and important lessons we long to share with future generations. By writing from our deepest essence, we are creating our legacy of real value. We are preserving our most cherished ideals.

I think about my ancestors. I know their occupations, their statistics, where they lived and much of the earthly stuff of their lives. But do I really *know* them? Do I know what was important to them, what they valued and why? Do I know the deeper essence of who they were? Sadly, not really. I wish I would have asked more questions when they were alive.

So an ethical will, or whatever you'd like to call it, gives us an opportunity to share our knowledge about those whose shoulders we stand upon. It is also a way of conveying our authentic selves so our future generations will *know* us and *understand* the beliefs we held most dear. And most importantly, to convey *why* we built that moral framework of our lives. It is our true and lasting legacy.

We invest our time deciding who to list as the beneficiaries of all our worldly goods and riches. Why not give as much attention to passing along our internal, deeply held convictions?

Like the shipwrecked oar being repurposed as a railing, the life-long wisdom we have gained and our emotional and spiritual insights can be preserved and used by the coming generations in new and significant ways.

From my earthly vantage point on the shore today, I look out over the rolling ocean waves as far as I can see into its endless distance. Its vastness is eternal. Timeless. Everlasting. That's how far our legacy can reach. A pebble in an infinite pond. A never-ending arc of understanding. A meaningful inheritance to preserve.

The driftwood hut on the shore in the opening photo is gone now. Reclaimed by the sea. Vanished forever. Don't let this happen to your life's wisdom.

*************

*If you were to create an ethical will, how would you start? What is it about YOU that is essential to pass along?*

*I find writing letters to loved ones is an easy way for me to communicate. Choose someone today and write a letter.*

*At the least, what is one piece of your legacy you would want future generations to know and preserve?*

# Time and Tides

*"This waiting for the tide is a singular feature
in life by the sea-shore."*

-Henry David Thoreau, Cape Cod, Across the Cape

Thoreau is in Truro and spending time on the western shore of Cape Cod Bay. Calm and serene, these bay waters tucked inside the curl of the Cape differ vastly from the pounding surf of the eastern Atlantic seashore.

As Thoreau saunters the shore, he comes upon a fisherman's shelter which is a half keeled-up schooner. He rouses the sailor out of a sound mid-day sleep hoping to borrow his clam digger. The next morning, the schooner is gone, but Thoreau could see the vessel sitting in mud at low tide on a distant shore. The fisherman would have to wait for high tide to leave.

All day he continued to explore the western shore, noting "...the water was much smoother, and the bottom was partially covered with the slender grass-like seaweed, which we had not seen on the Atlantic side;"[14] Later in the day, he walked back to Highland Lighthouse to spend the night. Thoreau appreciated the peaceful ending to this day saying, "Just before reaching the light-house, we saw the sun set in the Bay..."[15]

Low tide on Cape Cod
173

## *Be Patient or Proceed?*

Sir Isaac Newton is credited with the discovery of gravity around 1665. By 1687, he had also discovered "that ocean tides result from the gravitational attraction of the sun and moon on the oceans of the earth."[16]

I have always been fascinated by the low, high and ebb tides of the sea. Here in the Midwest, our lakes are considered non-tidal. Our tidal changes, if you even want to call them that, are less than five centimeters in height. Our water levels change more because of the wind and weather, than the gravitational exchange of the sun, moon and earth.[17]

In this passage, Henry is noting that the lives of the seaman are dictated by the tides. Each different tide has its own "waiting or going" period. In high tide, the sailors must carefully prepare to maneuver faster and swiftly changing currents. Low tide presents the challenge to time a voyage to avoid getting stuck in the mud or stranded in the sandy muck of low water levels. Ebb tide, when the tide is turning around, presents its own unique navigational headwinds.

I titled Henry's portion of this essay "Time and Tides" because his quote reminded me of the saying attributed to Geoffrey Chaucer, "Time and tide wait for no man." I titled my essay, Be Patient or Proceed? because I believe we always have a choice. Let us look at these tides.

As I walk the slushy, shell-filled shoreline on Cape Cod, I watch the slow movement of the water at low tide. The timing of the waves' intervals is stretched out, crawling to the shore in no particular hurry. Low tide teaches me to be patient. Go slow with decisions. There are treasures to be found on this slower ebbing landscape. In these low-tidal moments, I use my time wisely and relish the calm endurance to proceed gently.

On a kayaking excursion on the Cape with my friend Joan, we witnessed the phenomenon of ebb tide. I have never before or since, seen the tide swirling while turning around. The water was in a gentle rotation moving from low tide to high tide. I found it mesmerizing. Joan timed our entrance into the labyrinth of the salt marshes perfectly. Marshlands are known for transition and change because of the continual filling and emptying of the salt water caused by the tides. Imperfect timing would leave us stuck on the mucky bottom, with hours to wait until high tide released us from the sandy sludge.

In ebb tide, I patiently wait and ponder. Ebb tide teaches me to give pause to what might surface from within. It tutors me in the discipline to value this time of non-doing and to use it wisely. To let things turn around as they are meant to, like the tides. Ebb tide gives me permission to linger and rest in this space of expectation of inner wisdom and new-found clarity.

Then, in comes high tide! Water levels rising, waves cresting as they march to shore, the energy of the ocean bursting forth. A lively spirit, high tide. Time for movement, action and going forward. After patiently waiting in low tide and my cautious approach in ebb tide, high tide beckons me to advance, like the green light of a traffic signal. "Go!" says high tide. "Onward to your next uncharted voyage!"

Our lives move in tidal cycles. We go through phases of low tide, ebb tide and high tide. In some periods, we linger in one of the tidewater times longer than others. Sometimes there are more external events happening, we are busy and life is full. Sometimes there are quieter intervals of internal transitioning. At each juncture, we learn more about ourselves and we grow.

The oceanic waves and the tides, are in constant movement. Stopping for no one. Time is like that, too.

Continually moving. Nothing we can do to stop it or slow it down. Like the tides, it follows its own rhythm. Tick, tock, tick, tock. The seconds turn to minutes, to hours, to days, to weeks, to months, to years.

We don't know how many "tick-tocks" we have in our lives, but someday the watch will stop. Whether we look back through the hourglass of our lives with sadness and regret or joy and fulfillment is up to us. Right now.

I love how Henry, at the end of the day in the opening of this essay, pauses to marvel at the sunset. To witness the closing of another day and the beautiful and graceful way the sun melted into the ocean. An appreciation of time.

We can use our periods of low, ebb and high tides to make meaningful choices so our lives flow in a purposeful direction. The tidal spirit of the sea is alive within each one of us, in rhythm with the timeless motion of the ocean.

Tick, tock.

*************

*How well do you function in each tide of your life, and can you find a rhythm in their cycles?*

*Looking back on your life, what or who has helped you move along on your tidal current to make fulfilling choices?*

*What tide are you in now and how can you wisely use this time?*

# Seeds

*"Vessels, with seeds in their cargoes, destined
for particular ports, where perhaps they were not
needed, have been cast away on desolate islands,
and though their crews perished, some of their seeds
have been preserved."*

-Henry David Thoreau, Cape Cod, The Highland Light

Thoreau wrote this quote while staying in North Truro with the light keeper at Highland Light, the tallest and oldest lighthouse on Cape Cod. On a beach walk, he noticed beets, carrots, turnips and other non-native vegetation growing in the dune sand.

Thoreau remembered the story of the shipwrecked *Franklin.* The ship, carrying passengers and cargo, ran aground near Wellfleet on March 1, 1849. On the ship was a Mr. Bell, who had intentions of setting up a horticultural business when the ship arrived in Boston. The ship carried a choice variety of nursery stock and because they were stored inside sealed oak barrels, much of the stock washed ashore. Thoreau writes this of Mr. Bell, "...and did not a nursery get established, though he thought that he had failed?"[18]

Me looking for seeds on Cape Cod shore
Pencil sketch from photo by Dee Beckmann

179

## *Lasting Blessings*

Henry continues his musings about this shipwreck writing, "...lamentable shipwrecks may thus contribute new vegetable to a continent's stock, and prove on the whole a lasting blessing to its inhabitants."[19]

Today, I walk the calm shores of Cape Cod thinking about these seeds of lasting blessings and ponder what message they have for us today.

A healthy seed can produce many good things. It can be a seed for fruits and vegetables. Food to nourish our bodies. It can be a seed for trees, shrubs and flowers. Beauty for our eyes to behold. It can be a seed of thought, understanding or hope. Sustenance for our hearts and souls.

A bad seed can also be sown. A seed can lack the proper nutrients for fruits, vegetables, trees and other forms of plant life to flourish. Those offshoots will be weak and frail. A seed containing anger, jealousy, hatred or any other bleak negative emotions, can harbor dark ominous underpinnings.

A seed carries the potential for life. The type of fruit it will bear depends upon what is in the seed that is sown.

As I watch my feet make impressions in the sand, I think about the footprint I will leave by how I lived my life. I look behind me and see the foamy waves wash over my imprints, never to be seen again.

What lasting seeds will I sow?

I walk further and think about the life of a seed. Tiny, as it begins its journey in darkness. Fragile, as it pushes its tiny sprout through the weight of the dirt. Alive, as its new shoot basks in the warmth of the sunlight and drinks in the moisture of the rain. Fulfilled, as it blossoms and shares its nourishing fruit with all of life.

Our seeds, too, germinate in stages. First, they begin in the safe garden of our thoughts. Then, they push through into sprouts of words, giving voice to that which grew within. Our words then come alive with action. And our actions manifest our seeds of thought into the world.

Are we sowing wisely?

Henry's opening story tells of seeds from the cargo of the ship that grew randomly on the shore. I think our challenge is to mindfully sow positive seeds, seeds of love, joy, compassion, tenderness, kindness and understanding. Seeds that will thrive and flourish.

We do not know where our seeds will fall. They may settle on fertile ground or on rocky soil. The growing conditions may never be perfect, but I believe within each one of us is rich soil. Our work is to tenderly prepare our own soil, so our seeds of goodness can sprout in any garden.

In his journal, Henry wrote, "I planted six seeds sent from the Patent Office and labelled, I think, *"Poitrine jaune grosse"* (large yellow pumpkin (or squash?)). Two came up, and one bore a squash which weights 123-1/2 lbs. The other bore four, totaling 186-1/4, all together 309-3/4 lbs. Who would have believed that there was 310 pounds of *pointrine jaune grosse* in that corner of our garden? Yet that little seed found it."[20]

We never know the magnitude of the reach of our little seedlings.

We may see the fruits of our plantings in a short time, or we may never see its blossoms. Properly sown, our seeds will sprout in magnificent ways, and it is our faith and trust that the seeds we are planting today, will bear nourishing fruit in their own time.

In the book, *Faith in a Seed*, Henry wrote, "Though I do not believe a plant will spring up where no seed has been, I have great faith in a seed. Convince me that you have a seed there, and I am prepared to expect wonders."[21]

Let us have great faith in the seeds we sow. Let us be patient and diligent as we cultivate the delicate seeds of all that is good. Let us expect the lasting blessings of the miracle of a seed.

Trust the journey.

*************

*What seeds are within you?*

*How do you prepare and tend to your soil on a daily basis, so its fertile ground can bear great fruit?*

*What one seed can you sow today with potential to grow into a blossom of goodness in your world?*

# Highland Light – A Beacon of Perspective
## North Truro, Massachusetts, Cape Cod
## September 15, 2022

A shark warning flag snaps sharply in the brisk wind blowing across Nauset Beach. The foaming surf is pounding the sandy shore on this sunny, 70-degree day. Ah, the crashing waves and the high sand dunes of Nauset. The place where Henry David Thoreau began his first hike to Provincetown in 1849.

The Thoreau trek today for Dee, Joan and me begins with food, of course – a seafood lunch at The Beachcomber, a charming seaside restaurant on the Atlantic Ocean in Wellfleet. We eat in the indoor bar area, a former U.S. Lifesaving Station. It doesn't get more Cape Cod authentic than this.

From there we travel to North Truro and the Highland Lighthouse, our destination for this Thoreau adventure. On his first trip to Cape Cod with Ellery Channing, he stayed here after a 14 mile hike from Nauset.

The Highland Lighthouse, previously known as Cape Cod Light, is the oldest and tallest lighthouse on Cape Cod. It sits on the Highlands, the highest and wildest stretch of Cape shore, in the town of North Truro and was built by the U.S. Government in 1797 and rebuilt again in 1857. At that time, more shipwrecks occurred on the east shore of Truro than anywhere else on Cape Cod.[22]

The lighthouse originally stood on a bluff 142 feet above sea level at low tide.[23] During Thoreau's visit, he calculated that it stood about 20 rods, or 330 feet from the edge of the high bank.[24]

Thoreau had a conversation with the lighthouse keeper about the erosion of the bluffs and the keeper expressed his concern about how many years the lighthouse could remain in its current position. These concerns proved to be valid,

185

and in 1996, $1,544,000 was raised to move the lighthouse 453 feet back from the edge of the bluff. It took six months to complete the project, and 19 days to move the lighthouse. A boulder with a plaque sits precariously close to the edge, marking the original placement of the lighthouse.[25]

We arrive at the lighthouse and approach from the parking lot, passing a golf course on the grounds. Progress? Unlike the rickety original wooden lighthouse, the white-washed brick and the attached stone structure renders a comforting, secure feeling. You can count on this timeworn beacon.

We walk to the platform near the edge of the bluff to view the ocean, imagining seafaring vessels continually depending on this light to safely guide them in all weather conditions. We are amazed at the close proximity of its original location to the water.

Heading back to the building, we decide to go inside and Dee treats us to the tour. Although the building is different now than it was when Henry first visited 173 years ago, I feel his presence. The stories he wrote in Cape Cod come alive in my imagination. Thinking of his recollection of the many shipwrecks in the book, I feel a newfound reverence for this beacon of life.

From the U.S Lifesaving Station at the Beachcomber to the lifesaving value of this lighthouse, my appreciation escalates for the daring nature of the nautical life. As I climb each black, wrought iron step up the spiral staircase, I think of those wild and tumultuous seafaring days. When we reach the highest part of the tower, the docent shows us a map marking all the shipwrecks. It is a daunting visual.

At the top on this clear September day, we can see for miles, including Provincetown. As I look out to sea, I think of the many mariners who continue to depend upon this lighthouse for safety. I learn that each lighthouse has its own signal of intervals of the flashing beacon, so that sailors will easily know their position in relation to the land.

*Joan comments on the perspective Thoreau must have enjoyed from this lighthouse. He wrote he could see Long Point at the entrance of Provincetown Harbor. His ability to see Provincetown from here must have given him clarity about the trek to that fisted end of the Cape. Lighthouses are that way, a beam of light providing direction and clarity.*

*We clamber our way down the winding staircase, holding tightly to the brightly polished wooden handrail. It is easier to descend backwards on the narrow steps with open risers, navigating the twists and turns of the serpentine staircase.*

*I smile at the gift of being in this lighthouse and I think of Thoreau's quote in* Cape Cod, *"The light-house lamps a few feet distant shone full into my chamber, and made it as bright as day, so I knew exactly how the Highland Light bore all that night, and I was in no danger of being wrecked...I thought as I lay there, half awake and half asleep, looking upward through the window at the lights above my head, how many sleepless eyes from far out on the Ocean stream - mariners of all nations spinning their yarns through the various watches of the night - were directed towards my couch."*[26]

*A beacon of safety, both in and out. A beacon of perspective. Sturdy in its conviction. A lighthouse - a lamp in the darkness, a ray of hope, a guiding light to show us the way.*

*Highland Lighthouse*

187

Thoreau

# The Journal, 1837-1861
## October 22, 1837-November 3, 1861
### Roughly 7000 pages and 2 million words

At the prompting of Ralph Waldo Emerson, Thoreau, age 20, began to keep a journal. His first entry reads, "What are you doing now?" he (Emerson) asked. "Do you keep a journal?" "So I make my first entry to-day."[1]

For the next 24 years, Thoreau kept a masterpiece of notes recording his observations, reflecting on his deep inner sense of spirituality in nature and logging his scientific research. I have been keeping a journal for over 26 years and I love this chronological connection to him.

I purchased a copy of his journal on my first trip to Concord, Massachusetts and Walden Pond. I immersed myself in his wisdom for three years finishing on May 6, 2022, 160 years to the day Thoreau died. I felt sad.

His last entry was six months before he died. In his final months he focused on editing manuscripts for his books published posthumously.

On November 16, 1850, at age 33, he wrote, "My Journal should be the record of my love. I would write in it only of the things I love, my affection for any aspect of the world, what I love to think of."[2] I believe it was.

Me writing on the replica of Thoreau's desk at Walden Pond
Pencil sketch from photo by Dee Beckmann

# Dam It Up

*"Dam it up you may, but dry it up you may not, for you cannot reach its source. If you stop up this avenue or that, anon it will come gurgling out where you least expected."*

-Henry David Thoreau, Journal, September 16, 1838, age 21

*The Boatman* is a great book by Robert M. Thorson about Thoreau's river sojourns. Many of us think of Thoreau as a woodsman, but in this brilliant book, Thorson chronicles his time on the water. Thoreau spent every season on his rivers, the Concord, Assabet and Sudbury. He shows us a different Thoreau – a man of the water.

The quote above, as Thornton mentions, is probably Thoreau's first complaint about the river. There is a flurry of controversy about the building of Billerica Dam on the Concord River. Farmers would potentially be losing meadow land to rising water levels, and there was concern of the consequences of the changing levels of the water flow on the Concord.

During this time, Henry conducted his own detailed research of water levels, water quality and the impact of the dam on everything below it. He wanted natural rapids restored.

Pencil sketch from photo by Amy Schoepke-Maas

191

## *Don't Hold Back*

The photo for the pencil sketch on the previous page was taken by my dear friend, Amy Schoepke-Maas, at the Mauthe Lake Recreation Area in the Kettle Moraine State Forest. "Dam." The word we say at the end of every kayaking season. Here in the cold winter of the north, our paddling routes will soon be covered with ice.

But not yet. Today is a glorious 43-degree morning, the wispy clouds opening to full sunshine and the promise of 70-degree temperatures. A real treat on this late October morning as I head up the Manitowish River for a three-mile paddle to Fish Trap Dam.

As I round a bend, the stunning golden honey yellow of the Tamarack trees in full peak greet me. These are the only evergreens that turn yellow in the fall and lose their needles in the winter. The tone on the river is absolute silence. Except for the occasional honk of a trumpeter swan or the jolting caw of a crow, a hush envelopes the landscape. A lone dragonfly whizzes by.

I quietly navigate the reed-lined bank and approach the dam. The small waterfall next to the dam roars in sharp contrast to my muted morning paddle. I think I'll be going over Niagara Falls in a minute!

Fish Trap Dam is not the kind of man-made dam you would think. It is an oversized culvert used to direct the channel of water, with an above ground opening allowing access to control the strength of the flow.

The waterfall next to it, huge rocks with oversized tree trunks lodged in between, slows the cascading flow of water that tumbles down this small descent. There is a strip of land in between the two to portage a boat from one side of the dam to the other.

Today, the water is furiously tumbling out of both sides, pushing my kayak sideways. I am forced to retreat and go with the flow. No stopping at the portage area today.

As I rest my paddle on my kayak and drift with the current swiftly exiting both of these "dams," two thoughts occur to me. The first is the distinct contrast of these two interruptions to the water's flow – one man-made and one natural. Side by side. How often are the obstructions in my life caused by others? How often are they the result of natural occurrence? Either way, the hindrances cause a change of direction, so how do I process this course correction?

Interesting, I think as I begin paddling again. Today, this man-made dam is allowing the flow of water. But the real purpose of a dam is to impound water. Sounds prison-like to me. Yet, there are both benefits and drawbacks on a larger scale. One advantage is controlled flow produces electricity and distribution of water for irrigation. A detriment is if the dam gates do not open, water levels rise in the reservoir, flooding backwater regions, clogging the impounded water. Ugh.

On a personal level, what am I damming up inside? What feelings and emotions remain flooded in my backwaters? Am I afraid to open my floodgates to the potential of gushing outflow?

My dear friend Joan Anderson once shared a quote with me about being emotionally clogged. I am not sure of the source, but it is profound. It reads:

"If you don't deal with transitions or problems they…
1. Echo in your mind
2. Stay stored in your body
3. Get recorded by your emotions
4. Get inscribed on your nerves."

I am more afraid of those four consequences than opening my floodgates. Especially that last one – "inscribed on your nerves." Feels like nails screeching down a blackboard.

Returning to the quiet further down river, I submerge to a deeper place within as I ponder what has imprinted itself on me. Etched inside, both healthy and unhealthy scribblings reside. The yin and yang of joy and sorrow.

I continually need to open my own floodgates to release what has been neglected and is dammed up inside. I want my way forward to be open and flow free, not choked and suppressed behind my self-made dam.

Henry wrote in his journal, "We have a waterfall which corresponds even to Niagara somewhere within us."[3] I thought I heard Niagara earlier!

Got it, Henry! I release the healthy emotions with joy and exuberance, and the unhealthy ones with gratitude. They have served their purpose. Thanks for visiting, I say to all of them, but "dam" it's good to see you go!

*************

*What stuff is floating in the reservoir behind your dam?*

*What sentiments of the essay resonated and how have they imprinted themselves within you?*

*What floodgate did you open for yourself today?*

194

## Kayaking the Confluence
### Concord, Massachusetts
### June 2, 2021

A sunny, 67-degree day greets us as we head to Concord, Massachusetts, to kayak the three rivers that meet at the confluence of Egg Rock, "the rock feature where the Sudbury and Assabet Rivers flow together to form the Concord River..." This rock became an island in high water and according to the trail guide, Thoreau and Emerson enjoyed sitting on this rock, which appeared egg shaped when looked at from different angles.[4]

This area is prime Thoreau boating country. Prior to our paddle on these three rivers, I have been immersed in reading The Boatman: Henry David Thoreau's River Years, by Robert M. Thorson. He chronicles Thoreau's many adventures during every season of the year on these three rivers - boating, walking and skating on the ice, swimming in the rivers, fishing, researching water quality and depth. His family owned a home on the Sudbury River so life on these rivers was at the core of Thoreau's boating life.

I am so excited to be here to experience the current of Thoreau's river life. We bring our own kayaks and put in downstream from Egg Rock near the river bridge on Lowell Road in Concord. The sun's radiance glances off the river and the gentle breeze welcomes us on to the calm waters.

First, we kayak up the Assabet River, our intent to paddle a mile or two of this 31-mile long river. We veer right after passing Egg Rock and soon we see the infamous "Leaning Hemlocks" that Thoreau referred to many times on his river journeys up the Assabet. This river is more secluded, wilder and narrower than the Sudbury or Concord, and when Thoreau was in need of more solitude, the Assabet was his river of choice. Farther up river, the banks are graced with protected open land.

We head back down the Assabet to the confluence at Egg Rock and I take a photo of a partially legible inscription on one of the rocks, inscribed in 1885, honoring and celebrating the 250th anniversary of the founding of Concord. The complete message chiseled into the rock pays tribute to the Native Americans and reads, "On the hill Nashawtuck at the meeting of the rivers and along the banks lived the Indian owners of Musketaquid before the white men came."[5]

Around Egg Rock and to the right we paddle on, now on the Sudbury River. The Sudbury is a wider 32.7-mile tributary of the Concord River, flowing parallel to Main Street in Concord. Thoreau's family home was on this riverbank. We paddle past Nashawtuck Bridge, built of magnificent stone in 1883, my pencil sketch for this essay, and then stop for our lunch break. We back into a marshy area, the former Thoreau residence in view, and enjoy our peanut butter sandwiches. I feel a sacredness here, knowing that Thoreau's time on these rivers was meaningful and fun.

The Great Meadows area here that Henry loved lines the banks of the Concord and Sudbury Rivers. Seasonally, this section of river wetlands floods, which created an expanded waterway for his boating excursions. Now called the Great Meadows National Wildlife Refuge, Thoreau would love knowing his precious waters and lands are protected. I look over the expanse of these meadows and think about the intimate exploring and unending discovery he experienced.

After lunch, we head back towards the confluence, again turn to the right and we are now on the Concord River. As we paddle the river, we come to Old North Bridge, the historic site of the first day of the American Revolutionary War. This first instance of American militia turning back the British still stands as one of the most significant events in American history, and prompted Emerson to note it as "the shot heard round the world."[6]

We kayak back to our boat landing after passing under Old North Bridge again, and I ponder the differences of these rivers: Assabet, wilder and more primitive and attune to nature; Sudbury, expansive and full of meadows and fields on one side, and rows of homes on the other; Concord, a bigger, busier river full of history, flowing 15 miles north to meet the Merrimack River in Lowell, Massachusetts.

Today is a very special day for me. Although we paddled a few short miles up and down each river, I feel the time spent here echoed Henry's entire lifetime. His love of these rivers and the confluence endeared him to the intimacy of these three waterways. His inquisitiveness led him to research and learn everything he could about them, and how they related to us. And his love of the significance of nature and man encouraged him to write it all down, so that future generations would know what he had come to learn.

*Approaching the 1883 stone
Nashawtuck Bridge near Thoreau's home*

200

# The Tight Ship

*"I am struck by the fact that no work has been shirked when a piece of cloth is produced, every thread has been counted in the finest web...The arts teach us a thousand lessons. Not a yard of cloth can be woven without the most thorough fidelity in the weaver. The ship must be made absolutely tight before it is launched."*

-Henry David Thoreau, Journal, January, 1851, Age 33

Thoreau writes this quote in the winter. He takes his walks to frozen Walden Pond and strolls across the Great Meadows on the crusty snow.

In *The Boatman,* Thorson refers to a letter Thoreau wrote to his friend, Charles Wyatt Rice, on August 5, 1836, when he was home on leave from college. In the letter, Thoreau writes that he "was building a boat to 'keep soul and body together.'" Was he talking about a physical boat, of which he built three in his lifetime, or was he talking about himself?

After graduating from college in 1837, he unofficially changed his name from David Henry, his birth name, to Henry David. He decided he had become a new man, beginning a new chapter in his life.

Physical and spiritual buoyancy

201

## *Buoyancy*

I absolutely love Henry's opening quote for the duality of pondering. "Fidelity in the weaver," has a two-fold meaning for me.

First, fidelity is defined as faithfulness to a person, cause or belief, demonstrated by loyalty and support.[7] Essential to Thoreau, if he were going to build a tight ship and bring soul and body together, was the inherent moral character of a person.

Fidelity, in another definition refers to the degree of exactness with which something is copied or reproduced.[8] Thus, his reference to the cloth that the weaver is creating. Both, weaver and cloth must be in harmony, in integrity. Soul and body. A tight ship.

As I paddle in the open waters of the lake this morning, looking down at my sleek little red vessel, I am buoyant on the water. My "tight ship" stays afloat because of the integrity of its structural elements. The hull, the strongest part of any ship, is the watertight enclosure[9] keeping me and my little stash of cargo safe. Made structurally sound with the right materials, it keeps me afloat and provides a consistency, a balance to my paddling. It keeps me upright and moving forward. I am the weaver, the kayak is my cloth.

A propeller or the engines of a ship are critical to its reliability and ability to move forward. Without a properly working system of propulsion, a ship cannot move. My body, using my arms in balanced rhythm with my paddle, is my modus operandi, and must be in good working order if I am to keep paddlin' on.

A navigation area is critical to a well-functioning tight ship. The ship's bridge is its command center, continually monitoring its course. My "command center" is me! Looking around, I am mindful of what is happening on the lake and I carefully navigate my little tight ship in the direction I intend to go.

You know where I'm going with this, right?

I have used this saying for many years: "The answers are always in your own boat." Notice I said, "OWN boat." Not anyone else's boat, not on the water, not because of the weather. Your own vessel, your own tight ship.

There are many things that are outside of our boats – family, friends, work, finances, activities, expectations, obligations and so much more. But what is inside our boats propels us forward and keeps us buoyant in the current of living a meaningful life.

The center of a boat is its weakest point,[10] so it is critical to safely secure our inner abundance, our core in the cockpit of our boat. Henry believed in the importance of the individual, and by taking care of ourselves, society as a whole is healthier. Who we are matters. When we empower ourselves, we empower others.

When each of our ships is upright and intact, we can all sail together in a happy flotilla. We are not battleships fighting each other. We are not sinking or sending an SOS signal to be rescued. We are triumphantly navigating our own course, and are strong enough to help others in distress.

In the flurry of our hectic lifestyle, what is urgent takes precedence over what is important. We often think the important things will get taken care of after the urgent ones. But guess what? There are always urgent things.

So it's important to routinely check our ship, to discern what keeps us afloat no matter the calmness or turbulence of our waters. I strongly believe, there are two

203

essentials that always belong in our boats – self-acceptance and gratitude. These are the strong, structural elements on which the others can float. The elements of fidelity – true-heartedness, honesty, sincerity, integrity, truthfulness – can be combined with confidence, self-esteem, hope, joy, creativity and love. Whatever brings you inner harmony tightens your ship so it can be both physically and spiritually buoyant.

The time to begin is now. This year I will be 68 years old. If I live to 90, I have 22 years left, or only 8,030 days! Yikes! The current is moving swifter than I'd like. I challenge you to do your own math!

To tighten my ship, I routinely examine my hull to ensure my propulsion is healthy and strong. I re-evaluate my navigation so it is accurately and precisely on course with what belongs in my boat.

The answers are always in your OWN boat. Never forget that. You are the weaver, your boat is your cloth.

The buoyancy of your life depends on it.

*************

*Is your hull in need of repair? What should you do to reinforce the structural elements of your life?*

*Is your propulsion strong? Are you on a healthy course for mind, body and spirit?*

*Is your command center guiding you in the flow of a fulfilling and meaningful life?*

# Mansion of the Air

*"It is remarkable how large a mansion of the air you can explore with your ears in the still morning by the waterside."*

-Henry David Thoreau, Journal, April 6, 1856, age 38

On this journal date, Thoreau is living at the family house and is sauntering about in nearby woods and on the shores of local waters. In the days before and after writing this quote, he is journaling about spring and its welcoming sounds. He references the sound of the rain on the roof, the first since Christmas Day. He notes the voices of the crows, and an eagle or a fish hawk.

Sitting on a warm bank, he hears the peep of the Hyla, a green tree frog, and comments, "He is the first of his race to awaken to the new year and pierce the solitudes with his voice."[11]

A few days later, during a rainy, raw April morning, he hears a robin singing. His full attention is on the sounds of nature that are coming alive at this time.

Oceanside mansion of the air

207

# The Art of Listening

In an excerpt from *Walden* about visitors, Henry writes, "One inconvenience I sometimes experienced in so small a house, the difficulty of getting to a sufficient distance from my guest when we began to utter the big thoughts in big words. You want room for your thoughts to get into sailing trim and run a course or two before they make their port." What an expansive thought.

He continues, "Also, our sentences wanted room to unfold and form their columns in the interval. Individuals, like nations, must have suitable broad and natural boundaries, even a considerable neutral ground, between them. I have found it a singular luxury to talk across the pond to a companion on the opposite side."[12]

According to Henry, a mansion of air is essential, providing the ideal conditions for open and honest communication.

I find that to be true while kayaking with others. I learn more about people's deepest thoughts and inner feelings while paddling with them. The combination of the elemental connection to the water and the open air and space between us as we paddle, allows for courageous conversation. We ponder, then share.

I read once that one of the greatest gifts we can give each other is rapt attention. On the water in our kayaks, attentive listening flourishes more than in any other place I have encountered.

How often, in our lives today, do we give others our full and undivided attention? Distractions abound. We communicate with each while focused on other things.

Are we deeply conversing? There is a distinct difference between hearing and listening. According to Merriam-

Webster, *hearing* is "the process, function or power of perceiving sound; specifically: the special sense by which noises and tones are received as stimuli." *Listening,* on the other hand, means "to pay attention to sound; to hear something with thoughtful attention; and to give consideration."

So, it seems to me hearing is perceiving sounds through my ears. Just letting the sounds in, while listening, requires concentration to understand what I hear.

The true art of listening seems to be bypassed in the fast lane of today's society. How often are we only hearing what others are saying and not really paying attention, because we are thinking about something else? Or perhaps our phone 'pings' and we are now thinking about who might be texting us. Or the person says something and we begin to process our answer before they are finished speaking. We have become very distracted these days.

Our mansion of air on the water, whether it is on an ocean, lake, river or stream, allows us the vastness "across the pond," as Henry says. Our innermost thoughts have room to flow between two people, or more, who are paddling side by side.

Henry illustrates the importance of consciously listening to one another in this quote: "The greatest compliment that was ever paid me was when one asked me what I *thought*, and attended to my answer."[13]

The soft sounds of nature are not distractions, but provide the necessary background for direct, honest communication and rapt listening. Especially in the subtle quiet and gentle stillness of the morning.

In the silence of nature, we also listen to ourselves. In our efforts to give others our undivided attention, we need the same. Listening to deeper messages just beneath our surface brings us much needed insight and wisdom. We owe it to ourselves to be attentive to this soft, quiet voice within.

In your day today, try to notice the difference in how you either "hear" or "listen" to people and to yourself.

Listening is a lost art longing to return.

*************

*How can you bring the art of listening back into your life with a small effort each day?*

*Do you deeply listen to others, or are you pacifying them?*

*Think of how you feel when someone does not listen to you. How does it make you feel?*

211

# I Walk Alone

*"I walk alone. My heart is full.*
*Feelings impede the current of my thoughts."*

*-Henry David Thoreau, Journal, June 11, 1855, Age 37*

This journal entry actually starts out, "What if we feel a yearning to which no breast answers?"[14] This entire journal entry is filled with a bittersweet and melancholy tone. He is longing for the next direction of his life, looking for the company of others, but finding no solace.

He writes, "I am tired of frivolous society... I would fain walk on the deep waters, but my companions will only walk on shallows and puddles."[15]

He even searches his faithful companion nature, writing, "I knock on the earth for my friend. I expect to meet him at every turn; but no friend appears..."[16]

Thoreau is a man of his own convictions, not bothered by being a person on the edge of society. He likes walking alone. Yet this entry struck me how conflicted feelings seemed to trouble him. Gifts of solitude fill his heart, but his separateness also brings uncharacteristic loneliness.

In a journal entry three months later he notes, "Now after four or five months of invalidity and worthlessness, I begin to feel some stirrings of life in me."[17] Wow.

Solo Soarer

213

## *Solitude*

I chose this quote from Henry's journal because I believe in the value of solitude, but also because this entry showed me a different man. He is distressed in his aloneness, which he loves, and is struggling to validate himself, searching for answers outside of himself. Something he is not normally prone to do.

It is the ebb and flow of life, really. Often an unsettling and barren landscape. There are times in my life when I can fully resonate with his feeling of being unable to relate to anyone. I look for solace from others, but ultimately I return to solitude.

Especially on the water. I love kayaking with others, but I must admit, when I need to recharge, paddling solo is my most treasured time. I find more clarity, renewed energy and I clear out all my mental clutter alone. I have fabulous paddling companions, solitude being one of them. I am grateful that I love myself because who do I spend 24/7 with? Me! Feeling lonely is rare for me.

There is a difference between loneliness and solitude. Loneliness is a quarantine, a secluded place of isolation. We can feel a lonely disconnection in a crowd of people. Solitude, on the other hand, is a choice. I purposefully choose to step away from the ebb and flow of my life with others to be with my most favorite person. The choice of solitude is an uplifting time to get to know myself better.

As I paddle solo up river on this crisp, clear morning, I focus my attention on the birds, the way they are different. Just like people.

I watch the mallard and wood ducks on the water, usually five or six of them in a group. They swim in single file at water's edge and sensing a person in a red kayak silently approaching, they take flight together. The

Canadian Geese, too, do the same. It is impressive to watch them pick up speed in the middle of the river while maintaining their "V" formation. Honking jets on a river runway. Like social people, they prefer to spend most of their time in the company of others. I do wonder however, as I watch them continue their "V" formation in the sky, does the last goose in line really want to be in the "V" all the time? Maybe he'd like an "I" sometimes?

A Bald Eagle soars alone on currents high above the forest green pines. The dazzling brilliance of his snowy white tail snaps into view against the azure blue sky, like the flash of a camera. A Great Blue Heron, an imposing "prehistoric" bird, scours the bank alone then alights with commanding presence to the next bend of the river. I read that the Ruby-throated Hummingbird migrates alone. By doing so, predators are unaware of him, his tiny size protecting him on his solo flight.[18]

Are you a flock flyer or a solo soarer? Or a little of both?

I think about Henry's quote as I continue up the river. In a strange way, I feel a camaraderie with him as he struggled to regain his footing. He expressed a feeling of uncertainty in his search and I, too, feel that sense of unsteadiness now seeking my next steps. It was comforting to know that even Henry, someone so sure of his sense of self, could falter at times. We all do.

Kayaking solo creates a space to regain my footing. I have often written that in a strange sense, being on the water "grounds" me. It allows me time to clearly think about my feelings, to be in tune with circumstances in my life and to recalibrate my center. Being in solitude helps me make better decisions for myself.

I read that birds that fly alone have the strongest wings. They welcome the companionship of others, but do not need it.[19] I am like that. I resonate with the eagles, flying solo creating strong wings for myself. Yes, it feels empty at times and I miss companionship. Life is not a solo sport. We are tethered to our life team named "Together."

But as I keep a laser focus on the passage of time, I choose my teammates and my next steps wisely. And when I need essential answers I retreat to solitude, where I spend more time now.

I am of Polish heritage and I often lean back on the ancestral strength of those who came before me. I discovered a Polish proverb that says, *"Orły latają samotnie, tylko barany chodzą stadami."* Got that? It means "eagles fly alone; only sheep walk in herds."[20]

I take that as an ancestral cue to keep walking my path and keep soaring. Keep paddlin' on, as I always say, and trust the journey wherever it leads. And keep my trustworthy companion, solitude, by my side.

*************

*How do you recharge?*

*What is more beneficial for you, time alone or with others?*

*Either way, spending time in solitude can be helpful. Can you carve out slices of time to be alone?*

217

### Summiting Mt. Wachusett
#### Princeton and Westminster, Massachusetts
#### Elevation 2,006 ft.
#### April 6, 2021

*As I prepare for my ascent, I write this note to carry, connecting Henry and me more deeply on this climb:*

---

Dear Henry,
On July 19, 1842, at age 25, you and your friend, Richard Fuller, set out to climb this mountain, Wachusett. You walked 25 miles from Concord, hiked up the next day and stayed overnight on the summit, and hiked back down on July 21, 1842.

Your quote from *Walden*, "...endeavors to live the life which he has imagined...,"[21] is with me on this climb.

It's April 6, 2021 and I hope to summit Mt. Wachusett in your honor, one of many that I hope to climb walking in your footsteps. Well, not the same paths, but close.

"Although a kayaker, the summits often call to me - to stretch, to grow and to become..."                                                   *- Mary Anne Smrz*

---

*Being a hiker, Thoreau climbed numerous mountains in New England. In July of 1842, at age 25, he summited Mt. Wachusett, the highest point in Massachusetts east of the Connecticut River, with Margaret Fuller's brother, Richard. He summited 13 years later in mid-October, 1854, with Richard Cholmondeley of England and H.G.O Blake. Being a hiker myself, I am excited to explore these elevated hikes of his, and walk in his footsteps to the summit.*

*On this cool, clear, cobalt blue sky day, Dee and I climb this mountain in his home state. Unlike Thoreau, we do not walk the 25 miles from Concord to the base. The hike to the summit is plenty for us. A stone stairway greets us as we begin the climb up Pine Hill Trail, and I wonder if we are close to where Thoreau began his ascent. The climb is beautiful, well-marked with sign posts and trail markers leading the way. I wonder how Thoreau gauged the best route to the summit. I feel graced by his presence here among the old growth forest slanting up the hill. In 2010, I wrote an intention in my journal to hike "Thoreau's Climbs" and here I am.*

*Also unlike Thoreau, we do not spend the night on the summit. He and Richard pitched a tent and spent the night with "a bright moon and a piercing wind" as he later described in his essay, "A Walk to Wachusett," which was published in Boston Miscellany of Literature in January, 1843. He wrote "the summit consists of a few acres, destitute of trees, covered with bare rocks, interspersed with blueberry bushes, raspberries, gooseberries, strawberries, moss, and a fine wiry grass."*

*Are we on the same mountain? A very different summit greets us. A wooden platform with signs indicating the sights in every direction. Informational signage about the treasured trees and what to see and do in the Wachusett Mountain State Reservation. A fire tower. A cell phone tower. I think Thoreau would have run away as fast as he could from this "slice of mountaintop civilization."*

*The views are magnificent, to the east the skyline of Boston and to the north, Mt. Monadnock, in New Hampshire, his most cherished mountain, which he later climbed four times. We eat our lunch of peanut butter on graham crackers, trail mix and an apple as we rest at the summit.*

*We take different trails down, a winding route on Old Indian Trail to West Side Trail to Harrington to Link and Loop to Bicentennial Trail. The meandering pace slows me down to relish time on this mountain in Henry's space.*

*My favorite quote from his essay about his excursion is, "But special I remember thee, Wachusett, who like me standest alone without society."[22] He was a man of his own making.*

*Thoreau summited Mt. Wachusett twice:*

1. *July 20, 1842, age 25 with Richard Fuller*
2. *October 19-20, 1854, age37 with Thomas Cholmondeley of England and Harrison (H.G.O.) Blake.*

*Pencil sketch from photo of*
*stone stairway up Mt. Wachusett*

# Snow, the Great Revealer

*"The snow is the great betrayer. It not only shows the
tracks of mice, otters, etc., etc., which else we should
rarely if ever see, but the tree sparrows are more plainly
seen against its white ground, and they in turn are
attracted by the dark weeds which it reveals."*

-Henry David Thoreau, Journal, January 1, 1854, age 36

Thoreau wrote this New Year's Day entry after five days
of journaling about a continuing, blustery snow storm.
He notes there were high winds during the night and the
roads were blocked and schools were closed.

The north wind was blowing the snow horizontally. The
drifts were as high as his head. Walden Pond was
completely frozen over. A winter tundra.

One day he went out snow-shoeing, sinking into chasms
of knee deep snow. After twenty minutes he attempted to
retrace his tracks, only to find them snow-covered.

Thoreau posed this question, "If one could detect the
meaning of the snow, would he not be on the trail of some
higher life that has been abroad in the night?"[23]

Snow or coffee?

223

# What is Visible? Or Not?

It is a bright, sunny, blue sky morning. No wind. A foot of snow on the ground. January. Winter. No paddlin' on.

The single digit temperatures tempt me to stay indoors by the warmth of the fire. The sunlight beckons me outdoors, teasing me that it is warmer outside than the actual temperature. Ahhh, the tension. The push-pull.

I compromise. I head outside and then inside to the warmth of the Boulder Junction Coffee Co. in town, one of my favorite places, to contemplate more deeply my intentions for 2023. My cousin, Lori, and I will be sharing our thoughts soon, and I want to be completely prepared.

I greet Michael, who works tirelessly baking goodies for the coffee shop and cheerfully grinds out the task of making coffee. His smiling face beams, his spirit shining forth, emitting a warmth that says, "Welcome!"

I order a cup of Blue Heeler coffee, one of my favorites. The milder medium roast, a switch from my usual dark roast, is soothing today. Outer warmth of the sunshine. Inner warmth of the coffee. Good for my soul.

I enter the back room and take a seat on the gray, metal chair at the wooden table. I run my hand over the protective varnished covering on the pine boards and I think about the covering of snow. After a snowfall, we say the snow has blanketed the earth. Why do we use the word blanket? We use coverings to make us feel warmer, yet snow is cold. An interesting contradiction.

Perhaps we say "blanket" because the covering of snow cushions everything, quiets everything. A sparkling white hush. We somehow feel safe. Protected. Nature's quilt covers us in softness and comfort.

Snow is made of ice crystals which have space in between them. The open spaces absorb sound waves, creating that serene quiet after a snowfall. Nature's blanket of silence and peacefulness.[24]

Yet snow is also the great revealer, exposing elements otherwise unseen. I see tracks in the snow, disclosing paths of small or large animals. Unseen when the ground is barren. The shape and size of the tracks reveal the animals' identities. I observe the depression in the snow where the deer bed down, digging a small hollow to rest. Normally hidden elements of nature are revealed.

I think about the snow, sometimes covering and often revealing. Two things that are true at the same time. How about in our lives? A tension exists within us, between what we keep to ourselves and what we reveal to others.

So I ask myself, as I contemplate my life plan for 2023, what needs to be revealed this year? Are there things that stay covered? I feel in alignment with Henry, knowing he was musing about the meaning of snow at the start of a year. A fresh start to outline intentions.

What is the dichotomy of snow in the context of our lives? We humans are a puzzling blend of endless contradictions as we search for our answers. We hold on and let go. We explode with joy in the company of others and relish the calm of solitude. In changing seasons of our lives we expand and in others we retract. We laugh and we cry. We feel love and fear. We express tenderness and harshness. We have many questions and fewer solutions. Can you reveal the answer, snow?

I sit back and look around the coffee shop again. I marvel at the way the sunlight is streaming in through the mini-blinds on the sliding glass doors, creating slots of light on the gray, vinyl-plank flooring. I listen to the low-pitched hum of patron's conversations, huddled together in the other room, muted by the lively country music playing in the background. We could line dance!

A hodgepodge of signs fills a wall above a section of the room where two overstuffed paisley print chairs flank a long velveteen, chocolate brown couch. I scan the quirky sayings and one proclamation stops me, "No matter the question, coffee is the answer!" Perfect! I just simplified all my life planning questions with a one word answer. Not snow. Coffee! Who knew it could be that easy?

I came to the coffee shop to contemplate my 2023 intentions, to read and jot down my thoughts. Instead, this essay about snow revealed itself. Funny how the creative spirit moves me in the direction I need to go.

I look up at the colorful oversized wall map of our area, filled with lakes and rivers, and I think about how much I love to write about the water and long to be out there. But wait, isn't snow made of frozen particles of water? So I am really writing about water, right? Just in another form. Perfect. I take a grateful sip of my Blue Heeler coffee, which according to the sign, holds all the answers to my questions.

*************

*What feelings or emotions do you conceal or reveal?*

*Is there one you keep hidden that might be healthier to express?*

*Do you need to do something about it?*

*Grab a cup of coffee and get your answers!*

226

227

228

# Let's Go to the Moon!

*"We are surrounded by a rich and fertile mystery. May we not probe it, pry into it, employ ourselves about it, a little? To devote your life to the divinity in nature or to the eating of oysters, would they not be attended to with different results? If the wine, the water, which nourishes me grows on the surface of the moon, I will do the best I can to go to the moon for it."*

-Henry David Thoreau, Journal, September 7, 1851, Age 34

For a few days before this journal entry, Thoreau's notes give us specific advice about the plenitude of life. He reflects on expression vs. contemplation. He writes, "It is wise to write on many subjects, to try many themes, that so you may find the right and inspiring one. Be greedy of occasions to express your thought. Improve the opportunity to draw analogies. There are innumerable avenues to a perception of truth."[25]

His entry on this day encourages us to live life to the fullest, continuing, "How to live. How to get the most life. How to extract its honey from the flower of the world. And no matter where we have to go, be willing to go find it. Probe the universe in myriad points."[26]

Tethered to the moon

# Reach and Soar!

When I was a little girl about 8 years old, I subscribed to *Highlights Magazine* filled with fun learning activities. In the back of one issue was an invitation to send in for a certificate entitling you to board one of the first rockets taking people to the moon. This possibility was incredible to me. My Mom, rolling her eyes, graciously paid for and sent in for my certificate. I had my ticket! I was going to the moon someday! I couldn't wait!

I was glued to the television with great excitement on July 21, 1969, (GMT) watching the Apollo 11 mission as the first man, Neil Armstrong, walked on the moon. I was only fourteen years old, but watching this mission unfold, I knew my time was coming.

Since that first lunar landing, twelve men have walked on the moon. Today, fifty-four years later, the current lunar mission is called Artemis, whose purpose is to ultimately establish a permanent base camp on the moon for human transport to Mars. And to put the first person of color and the first woman on the moon.[27] Me??? *Where* did I put that certificate?

My favorite monthly evenings are when the full moon appears. Recently, I had an opportunity to kayak in the moonlight on a clear night with my sister, Jan and our friend, Annie. Paddling in the dark was initially unmooring. Familiar surroundings indistinguishable.

As the moon moved across the sky, she danced in and out of thin wispy clouds, playing a game of hide and seek. Although we watched her glow intensify as she climbed higher in the sky, I was unable to clearly see the water. Feeling suspended, a dark, unfamiliar cloak of instability enveloped me.

To secure myself, I tethered the tip of my little red kayak to the shimmering reflection of the moon on the water by pointing my bow in the path of the moonlight. Instantly, I felt intimately connected to something eternal, yet simultaneously isolated from everything. An acute sense of awareness swept over me as though the gravitational pull of the moon somehow heightened all my senses. When she finally reached her full brightness in the night sky, I was humbled by her beauty and clarity. I think of those who have walked on her surface and fifty-four years later wonder, where *is* that certificate???

As I basked in the cascading moonlight and rocked gently in my kayak to the rhythm of the soft waves, I thought how going to the moon represented a universe of possibilities. Expansion and growth. Reaching for goals and aspirations that stretch us. Moving toward things greater than ourselves. Serving a higher purpose.

Henry loved the expansiveness of the moonlight, too. On a late evening walk to Walden Pond, he observed the moon shimmering on the pond. He wrote, "We do not commonly live our life out and full; We live but a fraction of our life."[28] Henry, in his musings, recognized we all have more life to live than our "quiet desperation." We all can "shoot for the moon" as the saying goes.

During my own moonlight kayaking excursion, I observed the glistening reflections as I lingered in my kayak. The intermittent flashes of wavy light brought forth the gentle whispers of my inner calling in the dark silence of this night. These soul-filled undertones softly gave voice to my next steps, nudging me in an unexpected direction, encouraging me to reach higher.

Somewhere deep inside all of us, there are moonbeams shining light on our darkness, illuminating our path forward. Our biggest challenge is to overcome our hesitation and muster the courage to heed their call.

NASA continues to heed its call. Since that first lunar landing, we have sent missions to Mars. The Perseverance, which landed on Mars in February of 2021, carried a computer chip to leave on the red planet. We earthlings had the opportunity to submit our names to be included on that chip. Of course you know I sent mine in and digitally received an official "boarding pass." I bypassed the moon and went to Mars!

A certificate to go to the moon. A boarding pass to Mars. I continually envision propelling myself on a higher flight path. Sometimes I hesitate, but then I remind myself if the trajectory is wrong, I can make a course correction. The lesson is not to sit on my launch pad too long.

In his journal, Henry wrote, "We believe that the possibility of the future far exceeds the accomplishments of the past."[29] He would be amazed today.

The Perseverance also carried something else to Mars, a message emblazoned on its parachute proclaiming, "Dare Mighty Things."

Let us reach and soar to do the same.

*************

*What one thing would you do if you were to reach and soar and dare mighty things?*

*What is holding you back as you sit on your launch pad?*

*How will it feel to blast off? Begin your countdown now!*

233

234

# Summiting Mt. Katahdin
## Baxter State Park near Millinocket, Maine
## Elevation 5,268 feet
## June 6, 2022

*September 8, 1846 – Thoreau, age 29, and his cousin George Thatcher and friend, George McCauslin, set out to climb this mountain, Katahdin. They paid three-dollars for a steamship passage from Boston to Bangor, Maine. The next day they went by horse and carriage north along the Penobscot River to Mattawamkeag, and then a seven-mile side trip to Molunkus. They began their hike on obscure trails up Katahdin. Due to inclement weather, they never reached the summit.*

*As I prepare for my ascent, I write this note to carry, connecting Henry and me more deeply on this climb:*

---

Dear Henry,

Although you never got to the summit because of weather, your attempts to "elevate yourself" and get to the top were an inspiration to me. Hopefully, I will reach the summit in your honor. I am sure it won't be surprising to me that I will agree with your quote about this mountain, "This was an undone extremity of the globe;"[1]

It is June 6, 2022, and climbing this mountain will be one of my most extreme challenges. It is a daunting task and I am thankful for this opportunity to see if I can once more, "elevate myself" on one of your mountains.

"Reaching the summit would be a great accomplishment, but it is the journey which continues to shape and mold me, and challenge me to continue to reach higher. To thine own self be true, in 2-0-2-2 is my mantra."

-Mary Anne Smrz

---

*Ahhhh, Katahdin. It has long been a dream of mine to reach and soar and attempt this summit. I have been training for* this climb for five months and now the time has come. Let's go get this!

Just as I began this book with our story of the bioluminescent paddle in Castine, Maine, where Thoreau took his first ocean voyage, I conclude with his attempt to summit Mt. Katahdin. From big water to big mountains, and all things in between, Thoreau was complete in his love of nature.

Mt. Katahdin is the highest mountain in Maine and the northernmost point of the Appalachian Trail. The name given Katahdin by the Penobscot Nation translates to "Greatest Mountain."[2]

Mt. Katahdin is located in Baxter State Park, over 200,000 acres of land donated to the state of Maine by one of its former Governors, Percival Baxter, who spent the latter half of his life and much of his fortune on the establishment of this park. His endowment allows the park to operate without state tax revenues and to maintain an independent governing structure.[3]

His intention was to have this area be "maintained primarily as a wilderness" and it is important to note this because his wishes for the wilderness match up so closely with Thoreau's thoughts on his time in the Maine woods. This area is known to be some of the most rugged country in the Northeastern United States.[4]

I initially contact Baxter State Park to inquire about the process of doing a day hike up Katahdin. Preserving the wildness Baxter envisioned, I learn we can only drive in to one of the bordering campsite parking areas and we must get a day pass. The rest of the way we hike in. I was told there were three types of trails to the peak - **strenuous, moderately strenuous, very strenuous** – quite a daunting selection. My heart skips a few beats, and I tell her, since we've not hiked Katahdin previously, we'll take the strenuous trail. My breathing becomes a little shallow.

She suggests we take the Chimney Pond Trail to the Saddle Trail and then to the Tablelands leading to the summit. A longer hike of 11 miles round trip, but the best option for Katahdin rookies, I was told. "Allow 10 to 12 hours to complete," she directed me and "carry a minimum of two quarts of water per person." Now I'm sweating. "Set a turnaround time," she continues. "This is your start time plus the number of daylight hours divided by two. Stick to it." This is literally no walk in the park. "Got it," I meekly reply and hang up the phone. Palms sweating, I am excited and nervous all at once.

In my Thoreau mindset I had hoped to follow his path up Katahdin as closely as possible. This would have us hiking up Abol Trail, one of the **very strenuous** trails to the summit. Not this time, Henry.

Thoreau and his traveling companions arrived at the base of Katahdin at Abol Stream, after paddling up the West Branch of the Penobscot River. They then proceeded on foot, which would be the closest path to what is now Abol Trail, bushwhacking their way up the mountain. Thoreau wrote, "We determined to steer directly for the base of the highest peak, leaving a large slide...on our left...Ktaadn (as it was spelled then) presented a different aspect from any mountain I have seen, there being a greater proportion of naked rock rising abruptly from the forest; and we looked up at this blue barrier as if it were some fragment of a wall which anciently bounded the earth in that direction."[5]

On the morning of September 8, 1846, they began their summit attempt. Soon, his companions were out of sight behind him, and in his words, "...I climbed alone over huge rocks, loosely poised, a mile or more, still edging toward the clouds; for though the day was clear elsewhere, the summit was concealed by mist. The mountain seemed a vast aggregation of loose rocks, as if sometime it had rained rocks, and they lay as they fell on the mountain sides, nowhere fairly at rest, but leaning on each other, all rocking-stones, with cavities between, but scarcely any soil or

*smoother shelf."[6] I am soon to learn what Thoreau meant by these observations.*

*We continue our plans. Not being Maine residents, we must call two weeks in advance to get our day pass. It is challenging to pick a day, not knowing the weather, but we decide on June 6th as the forecast looks clear...for now.*

*Dee and I arrive at Baxter State Park the day before to get familiar with the drive to the campground parking lot and scout out our trailhead. We take a few steps on Chimney Pond Trail and laughingly say, "OK, we hiked Katahdin!"*

*Back in Millinocket, we down a pasta dinner and hope to get a good night's rest. The alarm goes off at 3:30 a.m. and we are anxious to get going, but we are only 45 minutes away and the park doesn't open until 6 a.m. After a carb loading breakfast, we head out, arriving at the locked gate of the park entrance at 5:15 a.m. Our hope is to get an early start and we are the second car in line waiting to enter. The sun is coming up upon what looks to be a glorious day – clear skies, no wind, 36 degrees going up to 50 degrees. Perfect!*

*By 6:35 a.m. we are parked at Roaring Brook Campground to begin our hike on Chimney Pond Trail, the first leg of our climb. We sign in at the station, a requirement at certain checkpoints along the way. The trail is strenuous and rocky with an elevation gain of 1,425 feet, 3.3 miles to the Chimney Pond Campground. The surrounding terrain is lush and there are shimmering basin ponds, robin-egg blue from the reflection of the sunlit sky. It feels wild and free. Through the thick woods, we encounter few people, make reasonable time and are both feeling good so far. I think of Henry and can't imagine his challenge to attempt the summit through this denseness with no clear path.*

*Climbing the sacred ground of Katahdin, I think of the words that Edward Hoagland wrote in the foreword of the book titled,* Elevating Ourselves: Henry David Thoreau on Mountains. *He wrote, "...Thoreau loved to look up as much to*

238

look down. Upward and out. Elevation was a blessing, not a conquest." "Keep elevating, both physically and mentally," I tell myself. "One step at a time."

We stop at one of the picnic tables here and have a snack break and sign in at this checkpoint. From Chimney Pond Campground, the oldest in the park, the view of Katahdin is breathtakingly stunning and majestic. It is also equally daunting. We could sit here all day and admire the view, but we still have a long way to go.

We hike out to Saddle Trail, the next leg to the summit. A steeper climb, with an elevation of 2,353 feet, 2.2 miles, exposed and above the tree line. This area is different from the previous 3.3 miles, with more bouldering and climbing up significant sized rocks. It is a challenging and fun scramble up, and I now understand what Thoreau wrote in The Maine Woods, "...I mean to lay some emphasis on this word **up**..."[7]

Along the way, I continue to think about elevating myself. In Walden Thoreau wrote about "elevation of purpose." I think of that as I climb, although not too much as I must stay in the moment as I ascend over this rocky terrain. But I do ponder, "What is 'the next' for me? How do I bring value and calibrate higher?" Interesting questions, but the summit, for now, keeps calling. I focus and continue.

After clambering over a steep section of loose rocks, we come to an area called The Tablelands. The definition of a tableland is a flank of a mountain that has a flat top. The YouTube videos we watched prior to our hike indicated that although we still had 1.1 miles to the summit, this area was relatively flat. I think their definition of 'flat' is different than mine. The Tablelands on Katahdin, not as steep as the rest, still present quite a challenge to climb. Perhaps it seems harder because my legs are getting tired and I am ready for a rest. But not until we get to the summit, which appears just in reach.

There is an old, weathered summit sign at the top. I've seen pictures of it and this is the spot where everyone takes a gratifying photograph. I visualized standing alongside this sign for a long time and I include our summit picture here. We made it! Reaching this pinnacle was the culminating apex of the Thoreau journey.

I sit down on a rock and rest, and we enjoy our traditional hiking lunch of peanut butter sandwiches, trail mix and apple with peanut butter, washed down with an electrolyte drink. We summit at 12:30 p.m., six hours after our start.

The panoramic views radiate with beauty in every direction and are wildly stunning. "There is a vastness that quiets the soul," I read once and I feel that now. The sky is clear, azure blue with a few passing chalk-white puffy clouds, so close you can reach out and touch. Well, almost. Small patches of lingering snow dot many of the otherwise barren peaks.

I wish Thoreau could have seen this. Instead he wrote this of his attempt, "Sometimes it seemed as if the summit would be cleared in a few moments, and smile in sunshine; but what was gained on one side was lost on another. It was like sitting in a chimney and waiting for the smoke to blow away."[8] I close my eyes and in a small blessing, I dedicate this summit accomplishment to him, the Katahdin pinnacle he never reached.

We rest for a half hour, chat with the few summiteers sharing the peak, including one woman in her 20's beginning her solo hike on the Appalachian Trail and begin our descent. I would love to sit and ponder, but knowing that going down could take longer than coming up, we stay mindful of the remaining available daylight of six or seven hours.

We clamber over The Tableland's loose green tinted rocks, mindful of our footing. I think this is one of the areas that Thoreau would say it "rained rocks."[9] Descending brings different challenges. Our center of gravity is changed and we make a conscious effort to lean back into the mountain.

Soon, we approach the "slide" section of the Saddle Trail. This area is steep with scattered rocks of all sizes and loose gravel. Time for scooting on our butts! The safest way to go in this section…and easier on the legs and knees! When we come to the arduous larger boulders on this trail, we hike backwards, looking down at our feet to carefully take the next available step, while holding on to the jutting edges and tips of the rocky shelfs and crags.

I think we are making good progress down, until a young family, the dad with a baby in a carrier on his back, bound down ahead of us and soon vanish out of sight over a ridge. Ah, youth ain't it great?

I feel better when we meet an older couple hiking up and the woman said, "They said this was the easiest trail up? Are you kidding me?" As she huffed and puffed up Saddle, I smiled. "Strenuous" means different things to different people, and we're all out here enjoying Katahdin in our own way, elevating ourselves to the challenge.

Soon, we arrive at the Chimney Pond Campground and take a break for some snacks and complete our check in. The last, rugged, boulder filled stretch lies ahead. I take one last look back at the awe and splendor of Katahdin and think, "Wow, did we really hike all the way up there?"

The 3.3-mile return down Chimney Pond trail seems to take forever. My knees are especially tired, and I think I'd still be coming down Katahdin now if I didn't have my trekking poles! After a few hours of tromping down, on and in between these boulders, we arrive at the station at Roaring Brook Campground to complete our final check in. Daylight is waning. It is 7:15 p.m., 6 hours and 15 minutes after we began our descent. A 12-hour round trip!

We did it! I am so proud of us. Before our climb we made a pact, we either both summit or we both do not. If one of us felt we could not make it, we would both turn around. Yet the entire climb, neither one of us ever felt we could not get there. We took our time, enjoyed each moment and relished this awesome adventure.

I dedicated this climb to Thoreau, to elevating myself in body and spirit and to being willing to challenge myself. I am grateful for our safety, for our beautiful weather and this unique opportunity to summit Katahdin.

We feel good driving back to our hotel, too tired, though, to stop to eat. We fix ourselves the most awful dinner in our microwave at the hotel. What a reward!

I go to sleep that night smiling. How good it feels to stretch myself and to go beyond imagined limitations. To elevate myself, as Thoreau did, knowing the importance of rising above the conforming expectations of others. One thing I know, is that the insights from this climb will continue to reveal themselves for a long time.

For days and weeks afterward, Dee and I would often look at each other and with a smile on our faces say, "We hiked Katahdin!"

*The following week it snowed at the summit. How blessed were we!*

*View from Chimney Pond Campground*
*Mt. Katahdin in the distance*
*Photo by Dee Beckmann*

# Reverence

*"All wisdom is the reward of a discipline, conscious*
*or unconscious...Cultivate reverence."*

*-Henry David Thoreau, Journal, September 5, 1851, age 34*

Two days before this journal entry, Thoreau writes about
walking in drizzly weather. He notes that small weeds look
more beautiful than ever, covered in rain drops. "They are
equally beautiful when covered with dew, fresh and adorned,
almost spirited away, in a robe of dewdrops."[1]

The words he uses in the quote – adorned, spirited, robe – have
a spiritual dimension to them.  His journal entries around this
time point us in a more reverent direction. He writes about how
"our moments of inspiration are not lost" even if we don't write
them down, as they "have left an indelible impression..."[2]

He touches on the inherent sacredness in nature writing, "To
devote your life to the discovery of the divinity in nature..."[3] I
feel a gentleness in his writing at this time, shining a holy light
on nature.

His two simple words, "cultivate reverence" speak volumes for
a healthy prescription for how to live our lives in every way.

Sacredness of a water lily

245

# What is Sacred to You?

I love to kayak on Sunday mornings. Every other day, I am enveloped in silence on the river, but Sunday mornings have a deeper quiet about them. A reverent stillness. Even dipping my paddle in the water creates a noisy disruption to the tranquility that embraces me.

On Sunday mornings, I attend church on the river, sitting in the pew of my little red kayak. All of nature is in a peaceful mood, providing the perfect backdrop to cultivate reverence. As Henry scribed in his letter about mountains to H.G.O. Blake, "I suppose that I feel the same awe when on their summits that many do on entering a church."[4] I feel that sense of awe today.

My Sunday morning service on the water transcends the boundaries of church walls and religion. The fluidity of the river guides me in a stream of consciousness that is meditative and prayerful. The morning sun, breaking through the natural statues of the forest green pine trees, connects me to a radiant light as its golden rays meet the tip of my boat. A peacefulness wafts over me, like the sweet aroma of the flora growing along the riverbank. My senses are heightened by the sacredness of worship in nature.

I personalized the title, "What is Sacred to You?" because sacredness is different for each one of us. For some it is family, for some it is time alone, for others it may be living your life with meaningful purpose or serving a greater good.

Whatever it may be, I know one thing for sure. We protect and cherish what is sacred to us. We hold it tenderly, its fragile existence sitting precariously in our trembling hands. Our entire being shivers, feeling the ripples of profound responsibility to care for our delicate treasure.

I also know something else for sure. We love what is sacred to us. We love it so much we are willing to make huge sacrifices to ensure its safety and protection. We would do anything, including giving our own lives for it.

When our children cry out in pain, when we ourselves are hurting, when our meaningful purpose is in trouble, we care for their distress. We take immediate action, hoping to minimize or eliminate long-term impacts.

As I paddle near the canary yellow lilies, quietly giving voice along the river's edge, I think of Henry's quote, "Dandelions, perhaps the first yesterday. This flower makes a great show, - a sun itself in the grass."[5] He revered a flower most of us consider a weed, seeing it as a sun in the grass. I, too, admire my "shoreline dandelions" reminding me of the importance of respecting and caring for the sacredness of all life.

We all have our *individual* sacred things. And we also have many voices and live on *common* ground. Earth. We all have this sacred gift of creation to look after.

All of nature, our natural endowment, has a voice. Right now, that voice is screaming for attention. Increases in extreme weather, wildfires, floods, damaging winds, droughts and sea level rise to name a few, are an urgent alert that we are heading down an irreverent path. She needs us now to tend to her as deeply as we do for all we love and deem sacred.

How do we begin? Stewardship of our natural resources begins within each one of us. When we gently tend to ourselves, we realize how much our own self-care benefits those around us. It radiates into every aspect of our lives. We change in a healthy way, and in turn we change our environment. And that includes all of nature. When we love ourselves, we reestablish a vital link with others and nature. We fall in love with our earthly home again. We cultivate reverence from within and it manifests outwardly by showing a deep respect for what we value.

In 1987, John Hay, wrote *The Immortal Wilderness*. Of all his deep reflections, these seven words were all I needed to read. He wrote, "When nothing is safe, nothing is sacred." Written 36 years ago, it is a profound statement, unfortunately still true today.

Let us make the necessary internal changes to love and treasure each other and our earth to feel safe again. So we will hold our precious life tenderly in our trembling hands. We are not perfect, but if we take our individual steps towards sacredness, collectively we will cultivate a reverence for everything.

In the words of Henry, "Pursue some path, however narrow and crooked, in which you can walk with love and reverence."[6]

We must walk this way as if our lives depend on it. Because it does.

*************

*What one thing can you do today, to walk with love and reverence? What is sacred to you?*

*Whose life can you tenderly touch today with precious care? Yours or someone else's?*

*How can you, every day, cultivate this path of reverence?*

248

Thoreau

# It Takes a Village

*"It is time that we had uncommon schools, that we did not leave off our education when we begin to be men and women. It is time that villages were universities..."*

-Henry David Thoreau, Walden, Reading

In the Reading Section of *Walden*, Thoreau is lamenting about the rapid strides the nation is making, because the country is putting more emphasis on everything else but lifelong education, which is sacred to Thoreau.

He wrote this quote as he is recounting the dollar amounts Concord is spending on farmers and traders value and a town-house. He proclaimed, "Alas! What with foddering the cattle and tending the store, we are kept from school too long, and our education is sadly neglected."[1] He valued a core curriculum of lifetime learning.

He concludes this section writing, "Instead of noblemen, let us have noble villages of men. If it is necessary, omit one bridge over the river, go round a little there, and throw one arch at least over the darker gulf of ignorance which surrounds us."[2]

Pencil sketch from photo of Thoreau College main building

## Thoreau College
### Viroqua, Wisconsin
### November 10, 2022

*Toward the end of his life, Thoreau was suffering from tuberculosis, or "consumption" as it was called then, which eventually took his life. Upon the advice of his doctor, who thought the air in the Midwest might be healthier for Thoreau's lungs, he took a trip west to Illinois, Iowa, Minnesota and Wisconsin with Horace Mann.*

*From May 11 to July 11, 1861, the two companions traveled west through Chicago, across northern Illinois to Galena and boated from East Dubuque, Iowa, up the Mississippi River to Red Wing, Minnesota. On their return trip, they disembarked at Prairie du Chien, and went across Wisconsin via the railroad which ran along the lower Wisconsin River, through Madison, the Kettle Moraine area, and finally arrived in Milwaukee, where they boarded a lake ferry to continue their return journey.[3] Unfortunately for Thoreau, the trip was not the healing balm for his lungs he and his doctor were hoping for.*

*While tromping around his turf in New England, I was continually amazed that every place I went had a Thoreau "something" – Thoreau Trail, Thoreau Springs, Thoreau Bogs, etc. etc. Having read about his Midwest journey, I thought there had to be a Thoreau "something" in my home state.*

*Well sure enough, there it was, Thoreau College! I couldn't believe my find! The college is located in Viroqua, Wisconsin, which is in an area of Wisconsin called the Driftless Region. It is identified as driftless because the last glacial movement bypassed this area of not only Wisconsin, but southeast Minnesota, northeast Iowa and northwest Illinois, comprising 24,103 square miles.[4]*

*The gentle rolling hills and plush valleys, interrupted by meandering streams and rivers, are unlike the rest of*

Wisconsin, which is plentiful with thousands of lakes created by the glaciers.

Thoreau College is nestled in the heart of this area of Wisconsin, and is part of a movement of microcolleges across the United States and internationally. Microcolleges limit their semester enrollments to between 12-25 students.

By its own definition, Thoreau College is a "microcollege for the whole person. It is an innovative experiment in holistic higher education offering young adults diverse opportunities to challenge and develop themselves across all dimensions of their humanity. Thoreau College draws inspiration from the life of Henry David Thoreau, from the philosophy of Rudolf Steiner and Waldorf education and from the example of Deep Springs College (the first microcollege established in California in 1917) as well as from the global folk school movement and the traditional wisdom of the indigenous peoples of our own region."[5]

The more I read, the more fascinated I become with not only Thoreau College, but with this unique microcollege concept and I know I have to go there.

I send an email to Jacob Hundt, Executive Director, Board Member and Faculty Member of the college. I explain that I am writing this book and briefly share my adventures in New England walking in Thoreau's footsteps. He is interested in getting together, so we set up a time to meet. I am going back to college!!!

On a clear, blue sky, 64-degree November day, I head out early in the morning for my 10 a.m. meeting with Jacob. "When you get close to town, turn left at the driveway with the black mailbox, head up the hill, and you'll see our building," he instructed me. Easy enough.

As I drive through this area of Wisconsin, I wind my way through Mauston. I briefly follow a truck with the words "Rockin' Rudy" painted in white script typeface on the red

253

*back panel of the truck. I smile. Rudy was my dad's name and his love of the northwoods of Wisconsin is why I live there now. This morning, I feel his presence as I wander the winding roads through this driftless region.*

*The rolling terrain, even in the barrenness of November, is beautiful. The countryside is dotted with small farms and apple orchards. It is presumed many thoughts for Thoreau's essay, "Wild Apples," which he wrote upon his return to New England, were inspired by the many orchards he saw here. I like to think Wisconsin inspired one of his last manuscripts.*

*After a peaceful drive through these rolling hills and valleys, I near the town of Viroqua. I see the black mailbox, with its door for mail hanging open, a welcoming sign I decide. Come on in! I turn left up the gravel driveway, which also winds and turns until I get to the top of a hill. I park in an area by the gray clapboard farmhouse, a single building on six acres of beautifully rolling fields. As I step out of my car, I think, Thoreau would absolutely love this!*

*I meet Jacob outside and we head into the clapboard building, with its many cozy rooms and nooks and crannies resonating with old farmhouse energy. He sits down on an over-stuffed chair and I sit on the couch.*

*His first question is, "Why are you here?" I smile, a valid question. I explain in detail my "Thoreau journey" since 2019, how I am crafting my book and how I felt that a visit to Thoreau College was an important piece to include. We talked of our mutual love of kayaking and I shared the story of the Red Kayak Institute, which was my nonprofit organization for eight years, whose mission was to bring the healing benefits of kayaking to groups such as cancer survivors and their caregivers, women in 12-step programs and others.*

*He loves the concept and our discussion continues for over an hour. I learn that the college was founded in 2015, and residency for students began at the Thoreau House and other residences in the community in 2017. He shares with me that the programs are organized around the seasons of the year and embrace all five pillars of the curriculum – labor, academics, art, nature and community.*

*The Thoreau College brochure describes that in addition to academics, a typical curriculum might include:*
- *Manual labor at our farms, greenhouses, facilities or community partners;*
- *Discussion based classes in ecology, philosophy, history and spirituality;*
- *Workshops in the folk arts, homesteading skills, cooking, building, and more;*
- *Wilderness expeditions and solos;*
- *Participation in community celebrations and self-governance;*
- *Farm visits, local guest speakers and participation in the local community.[6]*

*An important strand, he tells me, is the Scandinavian influence of folk high schools. Back in the 1860s and 70s in Denmark, this element of learning was prevalent and is attributed to today's leadership, contributing to the fact that Denmark is one of the best places to live in the world.*

*At the conclusion of our conversation, he suggests an exciting collaboration. In May of 2023, a professor of anthropology from the University of Illinois in Chicago, Molly Doane, will be teaching there. I smile and I mention that is my alma mater. A serendipitous moment. He would like me to come back in May, do a talk with the students, possibly a podcast and that we must paddle the Kickapoo River. I am IN!!!*

*He asks me if I think my book will be ready by then. I tell him, "Jacob, you have just given me the inspiration to make sure it is finished." We arise from our cozy corner of the farmhouse, he walks me outside and we conclude with the promise of continued communication.*

I sit down in my car and exhale slowly. Wow, what an exhilarating experience. I leave the campus and drive through the town to taste its flavor. The shops, the bookstore, the restaurants - many of them closed now for the season - reflect the rich tapestry of this diverse community. I smile as I drive away, I am glowing, wondering where this unexpected opportunity may lead.

A few weeks later, I share my Thoreau College experience on my monthly call with my Salty Quill Writer's Group. One of my friends on the call, Tara, who lives in Massachusetts, is intrigued by the concept of this college. She researches it further, discusses it with her son, Hudson, who is of college age, and lo and behold, he applied and is now attending Thoreau College! I am blown away by the serendipity of how this has unfolded. We just never know how one encounter will bridge itself to the next opportunity. And I will meet him in May when I get back to campus.

One of the concluding sentences in their brochure says, "Through meaningful practical work, immersions in nature, conversations about ideas and literature, workshops in the arts, crafts, and homesteading skills, and participation in shared community governance, they (the students) have a unique opportunity to take stock of where they have been, who they are, and where their lives are calling them to go."[7]

I think Thoreau would have totally loved the concept of this college. Its philosophy completely resonates with his quote on education. "Henry's messages gain strength with time," Jacob says on one of our follow-up calls. Indeed they do.

I can't wait to be part of this village, and couldn't have envisioned a more fitting ending to my Thoreau journeys. Am I really going to "teach" at Thoreau College? Will I really be able to share Thoreau's and my thoughts with this younger generation, our future leaders?

Chills run down my spine! And I get to paddle a new river!

257

258

# Parting Thoughts

*"The rarest quality in an epitaph is truth."*

Henry David Thoreau, A Week on the Concord
and Merrimack Rivers, Monday

My friend, Henry David Thoreau, died from tuberculosis on May 6, 1862, at the young age of 44. He could have never imagined how popular his works would become, how deeply his timeless insights and wisdom would resonate through the years.

When his Aunt Louisa asked him in his last weeks if he had made his peace with God, Henry responded, "I did not know we had ever quarreled."[1] He peacefully accepted his death and his final words were, "Now comes good sailing, Indian and moose."[2] He was a boatman and a nature lover until the end. Though the town of Concord never fully embraced Thoreau's peculiar ways, at his death the town's children were let out of school to attend his funeral and the church bells tolled 44 times, one for each year of his life. His coffin was appropriately covered in wildflowers.[3] Ralph Waldo Emerson's eulogy honored Thoreau by saying, "No truer American existed than Thoreau. The country knows not yet, or in the least part, how great a son it has lost."[4] When I went to Concord, Massachusetts, I visited Sleepy Hollow Cemetery, where he is buried in his family plot in an area called Author's Ridge. He is there on the Ridge with fellow authors Louisa May Alcott, Nathaniel and Sophia Hawthorne and Ralph Waldo Emerson. What a peaceful prominence to dignify the stature of these prolific 19th century writers.

Thoreau lived a short but full life. In this book I wrote about the wonders of the natural world he experienced. But he also witnessed the devastation of nature. During his lifetime, damaging environmental impacts occurred as a result of ongoing development. Deforestation, soil erosion and dam building were causing decreases in wildlife and fish populations. "Thoreau saw how nature's suffering related to the systems structuring the world."[5] He felt the pangs of injustice - corporal punishment in schools, the nation divided over the issue of slavery, the forced removal of Native Americans to western territories. At the time of his death, the nation was embroiled in the Civil War.

As I write these parting thoughts in spring 2023, we too, are experiencing environmental concerns – wildfires and drought scorching the American west and other areas of the globe, severe worldwide flooding caused by powerful hurricanes, alarming sea level rise in low lying coastal areas and glaciers melting at an accelerating rate. We too, are feeling the pangs of injustice. Our country is deeply divided politically, the Russian-Ukrainian War rages on and we are experiencing societal inequalities. I share these points of reference because since Thoreau's time, not much has fundamentally changed.

That is what makes Thoreau's writing pertinent today, and his wisdom so valuable. He was controversial during his time, often going against the grain of the majority. It is precisely because of this willingness to walk a different path and to look for his answers, his truth in nature that he prevails today. Even his tiny tombstone casts a long shadow. An article I recently read sums Thoreau up beautifully. "In decrypting the living philosophy of Henry David Thoreau, the red thread that runs through his entire story is integrity. Being loyal to truth and principle was at the core of Thoreau's being. It informs his political actions and his philosophical lifestyle. Thoreau was an uncompromising force of nature; he did not let mundane concerns stand in the way of truth."[6] We can't either.

Today, we are benefiting from Thoreau's commitment to his daily saunters in nature. "Over the past 20 years, researchers have used Thoreau's observations of plant flowering and leaf emergence on trees and shrubs, bird migration and spring ice melt on Walden Pond to study how these events have changed since the 1850s, largely in response to climate change."[7] We are also coming to a deeper understanding of the value of time in nature, which Henry knew so well.

We sauntered with Henry on his paths and trails throughout this book. Today, research continues to emerge, validating the benefits of being in the woods. A new program in Canada gives doctors the option of providing patients with a free annual pass to the country's national parks. These "prescriptions" are part of an effort to increase access to nature and the health benefits to be found outside.[8] In *The Nature Fix*, it is noted, "In addition to its government-funded studies and dozens of special trails, a small number of physicians in Japan have been certified in forest medicine."[9] "Ecotherapy, including interventions like walking therapy and encouraging patients to get outside, is gaining traction as a means to help people tap into nature's therapeutic powers."[10]

We shared time on the water with Henry as we paddled his rivers and ponds. Today, water as a beneficial therapy on many levels is becoming more prevalent. Dr. Masaru Emoto's ground-breaking research on water crystals teaches us about the healthful properties of water. In his book, *The Healing Power of Water*, he writes, "We're created in water, bathe in it, cleanse wounds with it, and can die when we don't have enough of it. With roughly two-thirds of our planet covered by water and our bodies containing similar proportions of it, is it any wonder that it's such an amazing conduit for our thoughts, energies and healing?"[11] Other water research books reveal how the benefit of being around water reinforces our connection to the natural world and to each other. Research shows how proximity to water

261

diminishes anxiety, increases creativity, expands our compassion, and improves our overall well-being.[12]

As we summited the mountains with Henry, we stepped out of our comfort zone to experience awe and wonder, to touch the expansive fringe of wilderness. Henry understood the importance of this and in *Walden* he wrote, "We need the tonic of wildness."[13] Today we are learning that "these awe-inspiring events can produce persisting positive changes in attitudes, moods, and behavior, and presumably changes in the brain."[14]

I cite this research because it illustrates the incredible progress we are making to understand and embrace the value of nature in our world today. I smile because many of these books and articles include Thoreau's quotes. We have made great strides in validating what Henry knew all along.

My last reference is to a bestselling book, *Last Child in the Woods* by Richard Louv that spawned an international movement to reconnect kids and nature. His research led him to coin the term *nature-deficit disorder* to identify their lack of time in nature.[15] This brings me to the children. Just as I have reached back over the arc of time for Henry's wisdom, I now look forward to the future continuum for the little ones we are shepherding into this world. Bianca, Lila, Kurtis, Harper, Oakley, Crew, Addie, Millie, Teagan, Theo, Ada, Tessa, Noah, Warner, August, Amelia, Calvin, Juliette, Layla, Brody, Michaela, Max, Finley, Wylee, Faye, Natalie, Kinsley, Ashlyn, Vinnie, Grayson. A long list of beautiful names on my roster of hope - children recently born in my family and in families of people I love. I read their names and my eyes well up with tears. Their smiling faces express their joyful innocence. These precious little ones personalize the future for me. They motivate me to do my part to take care of nature so she will be able to provide the same nurturing and healing benefits for them.

We are their bridge over the turbulent waters of the past and present to a peaceful tomorrow. A tomorrow where they have the confidence to "live the life they have imagined" and "walk to the beat of a different drummer," in the words of my friend, Henry. A world where they can turn to nature for answers. We hold the sacred promise of a better world in our trembling hands. They are counting on us.

The closing quote of this book references "blue arteries pulsating new life now." We can bring new life into our unsettled world. We can find our universal truths together and live them if we are to be that bridge. Nothing can stand in our way. Life is not a competition. We either all win or we all lose. It's that simple.

I once read that books never end, they just stop in interesting places. "How many a man has dated a new era in his life from the reading of a book,"[16] Henry wrote in *Walden*. Books are a reference for a certain point in history, but their value spans across the arc of time. As Henry's opening quote in the Prologue says, "Books are the treasured wealth of the world and the fit inheritance of generations and nations."[17] This book has become my manifesto for goodness and tenderness, for love of nature, for simplicity and truth. Deeply instilled in me by my friend, Henry.

It is my hope that as you close the cover, you begin to live one new truth that benefits you, those you love, those yet to come and our sacred space, nature. And that your truth surrounds our beautiful world with a radiant arc of healing light.

Let us all begin a new era, paddlin' on together.

As we close our time together, I leave you with these final questions to ponder.

*************

*How will you now take these lessons of nature and incorporate them into your life?*

*How will you be the bridge for our future generations?*

*What will you contribute to the healing arc of light?*

*Henry's tiny tombstone casts a long shadow. How far will your enduring legacy reach?*

Henry's tombstone on Author's Ridge
Sleepy Hollow Cemetery

# Nature and Truth

There is nothing I can say that illustrates Thoreau's feelings on nature better than Thoreau himself. Throughout this book, I included my own insights and reflections. In this final section, I selected only Thoreau's nature quotes from his journal in chronological order for you to read and continue to reflect upon.

I call this Thoreau's Spirituality, because I know, after immersing myself in his life and his works these past few years, nature was the epicenter of his connection to all things divine and eternal. His journal entry, "to devote your life to the discovery of the divinity in nature..."[1] says it all. I, too, find my spirituality in nature – "the church of the blue dome." In the woods, on the water or on a mountaintop, the echoes of eternity resonate for me.

Thoreau found his answers to life's questions, big and small, in nature. It is my hope, with the writing of this book, to encourage us all to look to nature for our answers. The answers do not reside in government, institutions or organizations. The answers lie within the natural world, and being a part of that creation, ultimately within ourselves.

Nature knows the way

## *Thoreau's Spirituality*

"If a man charges you eight hundred pay him eight hundred and fifty, and it will leave a clean edge to the sum. It will be like nature, overflowing and rounded like the bank of a river, not close and precise like a drain or ditch."

*March 27, 1841, age 23*

'Some of our richest days are those in which no sun shines outwardly, but so much the more a sun shines inwardly. I love nature, I love the landscape, because it is so sincere. It never cheats me. It never jests. It is cheerfully, musically earnest. I lie and relie on the earth."

*November 16, 1850, age 33*

"As I could not command a sunny window, I went abroad on the morning of the 15th and lay in the sun in the fields in my thin coat, though it was rather cool even there. I feel as if this coolness would do me good. If it only makes my life more pensive! Why should pensiveness be akin to sadness? There is a certain fertile sadness which I would not avoid, but rather earnestly seek. It is positively joyful to me. It saves my life from being trivial. My life flows with a deeper current, no longer as a shallow and brawling stream, parched and shrunken by the summer heats. My heart leaps into my mouth at the sound of the wind in the woods. I, whose life was but yesterday so desultory and shallow, suddenly recover my spirits, my spirituality, through my hearing."

*August 17, 1851, age 34*

"My profession is to be always on the alert to find God in nature, to know his lurking-places, to attend all the oratorios, the operas, in nature."

*September 7, 1851, age 34*

"By my intimacy with nature I find myself withdrawn from man. My interest in the sun and the moon, in the morning and the evening, compels me to solitude."

*July 26, 1852, age 35*

"I love Nature *because* she is not man, but a retreat from him. None of his institutions control or pervade her. There a different kind of right prevails. In her midst I can be glad with an entire gladness. If this world were all man, I could not stretch myself, I should lose all hope. He is constraint, she is freedom to me. He makes me wish for another world. She makes me content with this."

*January 3, 1853, age 35*

"He is the richest who has most use for nature as raw material of tropes and symbols with which to describe his life."

*May 10, 1853, age 35*

"Live in each season as it passes; breathe the air, drink the drink, taste the fruit, and resign yourself to the influences of each. .... Be blown on by all the winds. Open all your pores and bathe in all the tides of Nature, in all her streams and oceans, at all seasons. Why, "nature" is but another name for health, and the seasons are but different states of health."

*August 23, 1853, age 36*

"I have come to this hill to see the sun go down, to recover sanity and put myself again in relation with Nature. I would fain drink a draft of Nature's serenity."

*June 5, 1854, age 36*

"Awake to day of gentle rain,-very much needed; none to speak of for nearly a month, methinks. The cooler and stiller day has a valuable effect on my spirits. It holds up from time to time, and then a fine, misty rain falls. It lies on the fine reddish tops of some grasses, thick and whitish like morning cobwebs. The stillness is very soothing. This is a summer rain. The earth is being bedewed. There is no storm or violence to it. Health is a sound relation to nature."

*July 14, 1854, age 37*

"The clearness of the air which began with the cool morning of the 28th makes it delicious to gaze in any direction. *Though there has been no rain,* the valleys are emptied of haze, and I see with new pleasure to distant hillsides and farmhouses and a river-reach shining in the sun, and to the mountains in the horizon. Coolness and clarity go together."

*August 30, 1854, age 37*

"Nature is full of genius, full of the divinity; so that not a snowflake escapes its fashioning hand."

*January 5, 1856, age 38*

"...be brave and hopeful with nature. Human life may be transitory and full of trouble, but the perennial mind...is superior to change."

*April 3, 1856, age 38*

"We must go out and re-ally ourselves to Nature every day. We must make root, send out some little fibre at least, even every winter day. I am sensible that I am imbibing health when I open my mouth to the wind. Staying in the house breeds a sort of insanity always. Every house is in this sense a hospital."

*December 29, 1856, age 39*

"After spending four or five days surveying and drawing a plan incessantly, I especially feel the necessity of putting myself in communication with nature again, to recover my tone, to withdraw out of the wearying and unprofitable world of affairs. The things I have been doing have but a fleeting and accidental importance, however much men are immersed in them, and yield very little valuable fruit. I would fain have been wading through the woods and fields and conversing with the sane snow. I thus from time to time break off my connection with eternal truths and go with the shallow stream of human affairs, grinding at the mill of the Philistines; but when my task is done, with never-failing confidence I devote myself to the infinite again. It would be sweet to deal with men more, I can imagine, but where dwell they? Not in the fields which I traverse."

*January 4, 1857, age 39*

"But alone in distant woods or fields, I come to myself, I once more feel myself grandly related, and that cold and solitude are friends of mine. I suppose that this value, in my case, is equivalent to what others get by churchgoing and prayer."

*January 7, 1857, age 39*

"When you think that your walk is profitless and a failure, and you can hardly persuade yourself not to return, it is on the point of being a success, for then you are in that subdued and knocking mood to which Nature never fails to open."

*January 27, 1860, age 42*

\*\*\*\*\*\*\*\*\*\*\*\*\*

*What element of nature – water, mountains, plains, woods – resonates with you?*

*How often can you get there?*

*What answers do you find there?*

270

*"I must now walk when I can see the most water, as to the most living part of nature. This is the blood of the earth, and we see its blue arteries pulsing with new life now."*

Henry David Thoreau
*Journal, February 27, 1860, age 42*

# Field Notes

This short section of field notes provides additional details about thoughts and locales used in this book. The significance and story of the book's cover, the visit to Thoreau Bridge, a Thoreau Glossary for unfamiliar words and a list of my Thoreau Journeys are included.

At his funeral, the church bells in Concord rang 44 times, one for each year of his life. I purposely wrote 44 essays, one for each year of his life, and added one more for good luck, like an extra candle on a birthday cake.

In the selected quotes for this book, he often uses the word "man" to refer to all people. I kept his text as written to preserve the integrity of his words. I did the same with the spelling of his words that are different today.

I chose Bookman Old Style typeface to represent the style of Thoreau's era, and a more modern look to my personal essays, using Trebuchet MS font.

It was my original intention to write this book, since it is titled *Paddlin' with Thoreau*, from the perspective of Thoreau as a boatman. Many of the opening quotes at the beginning of each essay contain elements of water.

However, as my connection to him deepened, I came to know him not only as a man of the woods, not only as a man of the water but as a complete man of all nature. So *Paddlin' with Thoreau* took on a broader meaning for me. Not just on the water, but paddlin' on in life.

His journal quote from March 12, 1853, age 35, sums up his life lessons for me - *"Dwell as near as possible to the channel in which your life flows."*

# About the Cover

The 19th century design was created by my dear friend, Ann Moss. The muted sepia tone and old style typeface reflect the cover of the original 1854 publication of *Walden Or, Life in the Woods*, as it was first titled.

The photo was taken by Dee Beckmann on White Sand Creek, one of our favorite kayaking waterways in Wisconsin's northwoods.

The black and white kayak on the left represents Thoreau and his musings from the past. The red kayak represents me and my thoughts in the present. He and I symbolically connect by the overlapping paddles.

The intricately constructed beaver dam blocking the boats' voyage and the wooden bridge in the distance allowing passage mirror each other in shape, but not function. The beaver dam is a creation of nature crossing the creek *on* the water. The man-made bridge crosses *over* the creek. Both serve a different purpose.

The beaver dam creates a pond for protection from predators such as coyotes and wolves and provides a place to build beaver lodges, which hold a stash of food for sustenance in the winter. The dam benefits the beavers, but stops our leisurely trek up the creek.

The bridge allows our passage over the creek, an arc connecting one side to the other, past to present. In the middle of the bridge we pause, gazing up and down the freshet at its elegant beauty, winding and flowing through the wooded terrain.

Both represent the evolving relationship of humans and nature that is intricately woven into the texture of Thoreau's philosophy and writing.

# Thoreau Bridge

The bridge on the cover identifies with another bridge.

Tucked away in the Hidden Valley Preserve in Washington Depot, Connecticut, in the northwest corner of the state, is The Henry David Thoreau Bridge. A 134-foot-long expanse suspended over the Shepaug River.

I was unaware of this tribute to Thoreau. My friends Nancy and Dave Vernooy, knew about Thoreau's Bridge and were excited to share a day's adventure. So on a sunny, blue sky September day, Dee and I hike the 2.1 mile Bee Brock Loop Trail with Nancy and Dave.

Before stepping on to the bridge, a gray, stone slab welcomes us, bearing the famous *Walden* quote by Henry David Thoreau, "I went to the woods to live deliberately..." Walking on to the bridge, we are greeted by the uniqueness of Thoreau's quotes inscribed in the railings. Phrases like, "what a piece of wonder a river is..." and "...in Wildness is the preservation of the world."

I stand in the middle of this bridge connecting both sides of the trail and survey the slowly meandering river, the sun glistening on the exposed, dampened rocks. I am amazed at Thoreau's continual reach and impact. He was never here, yet he is honored by the inscriptions on the railings. And like the bridge on the cover of the book, Thoreau's Bridge represents a connecting arc, trail to trail, past to present, humans to nature.

I peer down the narrow river as far as I can see. My hands, resting on the railing, channel Thoreau's quote engraved there: "The universe is wider than our views of it." He continually challenges me to widen my view and I hope the thoughts and insights shared in this book will help expand yours. I am grateful to Nancy and Dave for the gift of this day.

# Inscriptions on
# The Henry David Thoreau Bridge
# over the Shepaug River

"What a piece of wonder a river is..."

"...in Wildness is the preservation of the world."

# Thoreau Glossary
All definitions referenced
from dictionary.com
except otherwise noted

**Alburnum** *(n)* *sapwood; the soft, newer wood in the trunk of a tree found between the bark and the hardened heartwood.*

**Deciduous** *(adj)* *(of trees and shrubs) shedding all leaves annually at the end of the growing season and then having a dormant period without leaves.*

**Ethereal** *(adj)* *extremely delicate or refined; exquisite. Almost as light as air; impalpable; airy. Celestial or spiritual.*

**Firmament** *(n)* *the expanse of the sky; heavens.*

**Fluviatile** *(adj)* *pertaining to or peculiar to rivers; found in or near rivers.*

**Freshet** *(n)* *the sudden overflowing of a river caused by heavy rain or melting snow. A stream of fresh water emptying into the sea.*

**Miasma** *(n)* *noxious, exhalations from putrescent organic matter; poisonous effluvia or germs polluting the atmosphere. A dangerous, foreboding, or deathlike influence or atmosphere.*

*****Musketaquid** *(n)* *grassy plain; before it was called Concord, this place was known as Musketaquid, meaning "grassy plain" or "place where the waters flow through the grasses."*

**Penitent** *(adj)* *feeling or expressing sorrow for sin or wrongdoing and disposed to atonement and amendment; repentant; contrite.*

279

# Thoreau Glossary (cont'd)

Pertinacity *(n) the quality or condition of being pertinacious; stubborn persistence; obstinacy.*

Tesserae *(n) a small square tile of stone, glass, etc, used in mosaics. A die, tally, etc, used in classical times, made of bone or wood.*

*Musketaquid definition and meaning from
https://gainingground.org>our-story>indigenous-landacknowledgement>concord>gainingground.
Accessed March, 2023.

# Thoreau Journeys

Walden Pond, Concord, Massachusetts
November 27-28, 2019

Summiting Mt. Wachusett, Princeton and Westminster,
Massachusetts, April 6, 2021

Kayaking the Confluence, Concord, Massachusetts
June 2, 2021

Kayaking Penobscot Bay, Castine, Maine
September 30, 2021

Summiting Mt. Megunticook, Camden, Maine
October 1, 2021

McGee Island, St. George, Maine
October 2-9, 2021

Summiting Mt. Katahdin, Baxter State Park, Maine
June 6, 2022

Canoeing Prong Pond, Greenville, Maine
June 7, 2022

Summiting Mt, Kineo, Moosehead Lake, Rockwood, Maine
June 8, 2022

Camp 19, Boulder Junction, Wisconsin
July 30, 2022

Highland Lighthouse, Cape Cod, North Truro, Massachusetts
September 15, 2022

Thoreau Bridge, Washington Depot, Connecticut
September 19, 2022

Summiting Mt. Monadnock, Jaffrey and Dublin,
New Hampshire, September 27, 2022

Thoreau College, Viroqua, Wisconsin
November 10, 2022

# Acknowledgments

Writing a book, like any creative project, takes on a life of its own on its journey into existence. And every author needs a village to bring it all to fruition. There are so many people to whom I owe a deep debt of gratitude. Whether providing guidance in the practical mechanics of the book, or buoying me on my inspirational and spiritual waters, each person contributed value to the writing of this book.

Concurrent with the writing of this book, I felt the need to immerse myself in selected Thoreau adventures. I visited places in New England that were essential on his life's journey. I cannot begin to thank my Thoreau journey companion, Dee Beckmann, for accompanying me on these odysseys. We experienced Walden Pond, paddled his rivers, hiked his paths and summited his mountains. We created memories of a lifetime and enjoyed amazing adventures in my quest to experience Thoreau's life. I could not have done it without her. I am deeply grateful for her remarkable photographic contributions to this book and her thorough editing expertise. Most importantly, from the bottom of my heart, my deep and abiding gratitude for helping to bring this book to life.

On my trip to Walden, where I sat at his desk in the replica of Thoreau's cabin, I thought to myself, "I need a Thoreau desk!" Enter Richard Stewart of Boxborough Hardwood Furniture in Boxborough, Massachusetts. Richard makes exact replicas of Thoreau's vintage green desk, complete with the broken edge and the rough, worn-out key hole to lock the top lid. I had the wonderful opportunity to meet Richard at his workshop, and he gave me three of his hand-crafted wooden words that sit on my bookcase along with Thoreau's books. His intricately carved words are Thoreau, Walden and

Simplify, which I converted to pencil sketches and used as the headers for the blank journaling pages. Many thanks to Richard!

Every desk needs a chair. When my neighbor, Julie Engels, asked me what I might need for writing the book, I told her I wanted one of her small, wooden chairs with the woven cane seat. It reminded me of Henry's chair. She and Don graciously gave me this piece of furniture to complete the Thoreau ambiance. Who gives someone furniture from their house? Great neighbors do!

To my incredibly creative friend Ann Moss, I am so grateful for her perfect cover design. I so appreciate her tender care researching the original *Walden* book and crafting the cover to reflect its look. Her selection of typeface, color and design capturing the feel of a 19th century publication is amazing. She is the most creative person I know and I am blessed to have her in my life.

Early on, my friend Jo Reker sent me a clipping of a quote by Thoreau I used in the Parting Thoughts of this book. It may not seem like much, but just knowing she was thinking of me and sending a little nudge of support meant so much. Plus, I thought she'd like to be mentioned in the book!

Along the way, people sent me books on Thoreau which helped buoy me on my journey. At the beginning of 2020, my cousin, Catherine Borowski, sent me *The Daily Henry David Thoreau: A Year of Quotes.* Starting the day with his inspirations kept me focused on my writing during the tumultuous time of the Covid-19 pandemic. I am thankful she sent this book at the beginning of my Thoreau journey. Perfect timing!

To the Castine Kayakers in Castine, Maine, who took us on a late evening kayaking excursion into the darkness of the bay to experience the bioluminescence of the plankton, which is my opening story of the book. Their careful guidance and amazing knowledge created a magical journey on the water and under the stars.

During the middle of my journey, my cousins Steve and Diane Haraf, sent me *The Illuminated Walden in the Footsteps of Thoreau.* It is a beautifully photographed coffee table book, with inspirational quotes from *Walden.* I took it with me to read and reflect upon when I spent my night at Camp 19, my Walden without the pond. Heartfelt thanks to Steve and Diane for their support and encouragement of my work.

Speaking of Camp 19, my heart is full of deep and abiding gratitude to my dear friends, Sandy and Parker Sterner. Their gracious offer of a "Walden experience," to spend a night in their sweet little cabin in their sacred backwoods, was amazing beyond words. Our time together by the campfire was magical and the experience of solitude was just what I needed to gain a deeper understanding of time alone in the woods. The solitude at Camp 19 reignited my writing at a time when I was faltering. I profoundly appreciate Sandy and Parker. Their friendship is one of my highly cherished gifts, and I am grateful for all they bring into my life.

A special thanks to my dear friend, Gale Werth. I love that she has a "touch" in this book and most importantly in my life. Her little pencil sketch of Thoreau's desk quietly sits at the bottom of each journaling page. Our shared love of kayaking is so important to me, especially when she brings chocolate chip cookie dough! We have such fun! So grateful for her warm and caring heart.

To Nancy and Dave Vernooy, not only for the beautiful metal wall hanging with the inscription, "I went to the woods to live deliberately," but also for their support on this journey and our trek to Thoreau Bridge. It was a perfect connection to the bridge concept on the cover. I am grateful to them for our amazing and meaningful conversations and quality time sharing our lives' paths.

Heartfelt thanks to Pam Loring, Director of the Salty Quill Writers Retreat for Women. She provided a magical week of writing with phenomenal women on McGee Island in Maine in October, 2021. Here, I was able to craft the framework for this book. And I deeply appreciate the opportunity to kayak around the island!

Throughout this writing excursion I have been tethered to the wonderful connection of my Salty Quill friends – fellow writers I met at that retreat. To Julie Christmas, Andrea Kells, Fannie Koa and Tara Simmons – who have accompanied me and supported my writing with incredible insights and much needed constructive guidance. Their suggestion to include my personal stories, similar to the blogging in the movie *Julie/Julia* was terrific. The journey has been so much sweeter with them by my side and I am grateful to each of them. They are amazingly talented women who bring endless richness to the tapestry of my life.

Always a guiding beacon in my life, Joan Anderson has been by my side during each phase of this book. I am indebted to Joan, for steady guidance and for our courageous conversations about the challenges of writing and life. Sharing the visit to Highland Lighthouse on Cape Cod with Dee and I was such a special memory. My heartfelt thanks to Joan for always being there.

The solitary space of writing can be daunting at times, and you never know where your next burst of encouragement will come from. Mine came from my nine-year-old Great-Nephew, Bryce Ticen. When his Mom, Alaina, told me he writes every day it gave me the motivation to do the same. I thought if a nine-year-old can write every day, so can I. With pen in hand, I continued. With the encouragement of Alaina and Dan, he is a blossoming writer and artist. Thanks to Bryce, and I encourage him to keep nurturing his talents.

My dear friend, Grant Van Lishout, has been a timely inspiration along the way. His encouragement and endless support buoyed me many times on this journey.

Dina Casso and Jenna Richardson from my local chamber of commerce also gave me a timely nudge. At another lull in my writing, they gave me the opportunity to write an article for the weekly chamber newsletter. It was refreshing to pause and shift my writing to a local focus to regain my motivation.

My deepening connection to my cousin, Lori, has been a true blessing on my journey. Our rich discussions and valuable suggestions as we share our life's plans unknowingly opened the door for my Snow essay.

Often, books came my way adding inspiration for my writing. Dee's son, Bruce Beckmann, gave me *The Nature Fix: Why Nature Makes Us Healthier, Happier and More Creative.* It is an inspiring and encouraging book about the health benefits of spending time in nature. We share that love of nature and I am grateful for his support.

*Braiding Sweetgrass* is another beautiful book I received from my friend, Annie Shelby. What an amazing intertwining of science, spirit and story, as it says in the preface, on how we care for our earth. Our kayaking day at the Bittersweet Lakes, tromping over the portages and paddling the four lakes was tremendous. Surprisingly, the distances across the portages posted in rods, just as Thoreau measured, added an unexpected connection to him and new insights for this book.

As I was closing in on the book's completion, my friend Amy Schoepke-Maas sent me Thoreau's book, *Autumnal Tints.* Its unexpected arrival was a delight. That book was still on my list to read, so the timing was spot on. Her photo for the "Dam It Up" essay was perfect! Thanks to Amy for her friendship and loving support.

A note of thanks to Barb Clevenger, Dee's sister, for finding the perfect and amazingly detailed *Roget's Thesaurus*. And to Dee's Mom, Helen Pike, for purchasing it for me. At 97, she is an incredible inspiration for all of us on living a long and beautiful life.

My nephew, Matt Murawski, is always with me on my journeys in some fashion. I can't thank him enough for creating my author's website, and for valuable insights from his wife, Courtney. Matt provides ongoing guidance, helping me share my messages through my posts and blogs. Our connection is so important to me, and I am grateful to him for all he does and all he is.

I owe special transportation thanks to my brother and sister-in-law, Mike and Diana Smrz, my sister and brother-in-law, Janet and Mark Murawski and Dee Beckmann for schlepping me to and from the airport. Their efforts and willingness made my New England journeys possible.

To Josette Songco for taking the time to do the first pass editorial read of the book. Her detailed insights, comments and suggestions were invaluable. I can never thank her enough for her countless hours of review. Her photo of her dog, Daisy, gazing, was perfect for the Pause essay. She is a treasured friend on the waters of my life.

Georgiann Baldino is my ever-constant publishing partner for all my books. I look to her for guidance, clarity and wisdom in my continued publishing efforts and she never disappoints me. I could not do this without her. The continual current of her support means more than I can ever express.

288

To Jacob Hundt, Executive Director of Thoreau College, for giving me the amazing opportunity to share my book and Thoreau's wisdom with his students and staff. Our collaboration gave me the publishing deadline I needed. I look forward to meeting our future leaders, and paddling the Kickapoo River together.

I also have Cheri Sanderson, Boulder Junction Library Director and Pat Pintens, Spiritual Director at the Marywood Spirituality Center, to thank for the opportunity to do a book talk this summer. Their willingness to help me give further voice to Thoreau's wisdom is deeply appreciated.

For ever-present encouragement and creative nudging my entire life, I am indebted to my Mom, Toni Smrz. A special thanks for always urging me on as a pioneer. For her timeless wisdom of life's lessons, this book is dedicated to her. Publishing this book on April 11, 2023, is a special connection to her and my Dad, Rudy, who would have been married 70 years on this day.

On the other end of my family arc, this book is dedicated to my beautiful Great-Niece, Bianca Murawski. As the newest addition to our family, born as I was birthing this book at my writing retreat on McGee Island, she is our future. Bright, shining and full of hope and promise.

Finally, this book would not be possible without the wisdom of my friend, Henry David Thoreau. His view of life, his invaluable counsel for all of us to live the life we have imagined and his love of the spirituality and sacredness of nature are enduring. Humanity is grateful for his timeless insights, detailed observations and lifelong lessons. We are deeply indebted to HDT for his remarkable contributions.

# My Thoreau Chair and Desk

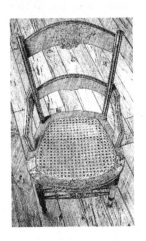

# Selected Bibliography

## Books

Bode, Carl, ed., *The Portable Thoreau*, Harmondsworth, UK; Penguin Books, 1977.

Bosco, Ronald A., ed., *The Illuminated Walden in the Footsteps of Thoreau*, New York, A Friedman/Fairfax Book, 2002.

Dassow Walls Laura, ed., *Material Faith: Henry David Thoreau on Science; The Spirit of Thoreau,* sponsored by The Thoreau Society, New York, Houghton Mifflin Company, 1999.

Dassow Walls, Laura ed., *The Daily Henry David Thoreau: A Year of Quotes from the Man who Lived in Season*, Chicago, University of Chicago Press, 2020.

Dean, Bradley P., ed., *Faith in a Seed: The Dispersion of Seeds & Other Late Natural History Writings*, Washington, D.C., Island Press, 1996.

Dean, Bradley P., ed., *Letters to a Spiritual Seeker,* New York, W.W. Norton & Company, Inc., 2004.

Emerson, Ralph Waldo, and Ziff, Larzer, *Selected Essays*, Harmondsworth, UK. The Penguin Group, 1985.

Highland, Chris, ed., *Meditations of Henry David Thoreau: A Light in the Woods,* Berkeley, CA, Wilderness Press, 2002.

Huber, J. Parker, ed., *Elevating Ourselves: Henry David Thoreau on Mountains; The Spirit of Thoreau,* sponsored by The Thoreau Society, New York, Houghton Mifflin Company, 1999.

MacIver, Roderick, ed., *Thoreau and the Art of Life: Reflections on Nature and the Mystery of Existence,* Berkeley, CA, North Atlantic Books and Heron Dance Press and Art Studio, 2009.

Searls, Damion, ed., *The Journal, 1837-1861*, preface by John R. Stilgoe, The New York Review of Books, New York, 2009.

Shanley, J. Lyndon, ed., Thoreau, Henry David, *Walden, (The Illustrated Walden),* The Gleason Collection; Princeton, Princeton University Press, 1973.

Spenard LaRusso, Carol, ed., *The Green Thoreau,* The Classic Wisdom Collection, San Rafael, CA: New World Library, 1992.

Thoreau, Henry David, *Autumnal Tints,* Bedford, MA, Applewood Books, 1996.

Thoreau, Henry David, and Peck, Daniel H., ed., *A Week on the Concord and Merrimack Rivers*, New York, Penguin Books, 1998.

Thoreau, Henry David, *Cape Cod,* 138 reviews, Author: Henry David Thoreau, Summary: Thoreau writes ten essays about the relationship between the shore and the sea; Print Book, English, 1987; Edition: View all formats and editions; Publisher: Penguin Books, New York, 1987.

Thoreau, Henry David, *The Maine Woods*, introduction by Edward Hoagland, New York, Penguin Books, 1988.

Thoreau, Henry David, *Walking,* Bedford, MA, Applewood Books, 1992.

Thorson, Robert M., *The Boatman: Henry David Thoreau's River Years*, Cambridge, Harvard University Press, 2017.

## Articles

Bode, Carl, *"Life Without Principle," reprint in The Portable Thoreau, Harmondsworth, UK, Penguin Books, 1977.*

Barber, David, *"Thoreau's 'Wild Apples,'"* The Atlantic Online, (March 9, 2000).

Conroy, Thomas E., Ph.D., and Smith, Corinne H., "Walk to Wachusett" excerpts reprinted in the booklet, *In Thoreau's Footsteps, A Walk to Wachusett: The Thoreau Trail from Concord to Mount Wachusett and Back,* working with Freedom's Way National Heritage Area. This booklet was originated for distribution at The Thoreau Society Annual Gathering in Concord, Massachusetts, on July 13, 2012.

293

# Footnotes

Prologue
1. *The Maine Woods* by Henry David Thoreau, Introduction by Edward Hoagland, xiii.
2. "Henry David Thoreau," by Beth Barnette, Center on Philanthropy at Indiana University. Accessed January, 2023, https://www.learningtogive.com.
3. Henry David Thoreau, *Walden*, Economy, 10.
4. Henry David Thoreau, "About the Text and Suggested Reading," *The Journal 1837-1861,* ed. Damion Searls, xxv.

Stars on the Water and in the Heavens - *The Awe of Insignificance*
The opening essay's context is taken from *The Boatman: Henry David Thoreau's River Years* by Robert M. Thorson, 76-77.
1. Henry David Thoreau, *The Daily Henry David Thoreau: A Year of Quotes,* ed. Laura Dassow Walls, Journal entry noted, October 28, 1852, age 35, 146.
2. Henry David Thoreau, *The Journal 1837-1861,* ed. Damion Searls, December 25, 1851, age 34, 102.

*A Week on the Concord and Merrimack Rivers*
The opening essay's context is taken from *A Week on the Concord and Merrimack Rivers* by Henry David Thoreau as written in the Introduction by H. Daniel Peck, vii-xxi. The final paragraph referencing the story of his printed copies taken from *The Journal 1837-1861,* ed. Damion Searls, October 28, 1853, age 36, 232.
1. Thoreau, *The Journal 1837-1861,* ed. Searls, October 28, 1853, age 36, 232.

 An Eighth of an Inch - *Oneness*
> The opening essay's context is taken from *A Week on the Concord and Merrimack Rivers* by Henry David Thoreau, Concord River section, 10.

2. Thoreau, *A* Week, 10.
3. Ibid., 10-11.
4. "Understanding the Butterfly Effect" by Jamie L. Vernon, May/June 2017, Volume 105, Number 3, *American Scientist* magazine, 130. Accessed February, 2023, https://americanscientist.org.

 Decaying Tree – *Grief and Resilience*
> The opening essay's context is taken from *A Week on the Concord and Merrimack Rivers* by Henry David Thoreau, Sunday, 79-88.

5. Definition from https://freedictionary.com. Accessed February, 2023.
6. Henry David Thoreau, *A Week on the Concord and Merrimack Rivers*, Friday, 284.

 Lapse of the River – *The Power of the Pause*
> The opening essay's context is taken from *A Week on the Concord and Merrimack Rivers* by Henry David Thoreau, Monday, 98-115.

7. Thoreau, *A Week*, 101.
8. Ibid., 113.

 Fresh as a River – *Shedding*
> The opening essay's context is taken from *A Week on the Concord and Merrimack Rivers* by Henry David Thoreau, Monday, 98-115.

9. Mark Nepo, *Book of Awakenings*, August 5th, 257.
10. Henry David Thoreau, *A Week on the Concord and Merrimack Rivers*, Monday, 106.

Enveloped in Mist – *Trust*

The opening essay's context is taken from *A Week on the Concord and Merrimack Rivers* by Henry David Thoreau, Monday into Tuesday, 137-144.

11. Thoreau, *A Week,* 137.
12. Ibid., 138.
13. Ibid., 140.
14. Ibid., 140.

Glistening Banks of Morning – *Awaken to Your Gifts*

The opening essay's context is taken from *A Week on the Concord and Merrimack Rivers* by Henry David Thoreau, Tuesday, 155-157.

15. Thoreau, *A Week,* 155.

Summiting Mt. Monadnock, New Hampshire

The context of the history and geological descriptions of Mt. Monadnock, webzine, Monadnock Review, 1997-2002. Accessed February, 2023, https://review.monadnock.net.

16. Henry David Thoreau, referenced from his Journal in *Elevating Ourselves: Henry David Thoreau on Mountains*, sponsored by The Thoreau Society, ed. J. Parker, Huber, A Mariner Original, 1999, 68.

17. "Monadnock|Geology," updated by John P. Rafferty, Accessed February, 2023, https://britannica.com>science.

18. Sea floor reference Friday, October 4, 2013, "Monadnock: the peak that became a paradigm," Accessed February, 2023, https://altaontenterprise.com.

19. Henry David Thoreau, referenced from his Journal in *Elevating Ourselves: Henry David Thoreau on Mountains*, sponsored by The Thoreau Society, ed. J. Parker, Huber, A Mariner Original, 1999, 60-61.

20. Ibid., 59.

21. "Guide to Mount Monadnock, Hiking Mount Monadnock, One of the Most-Climbed Mountains in the World." Accessed February, 2023, https://newengland.com.

22. Webzine Monadnock Review, 1997-2002. Accessed February, 2023, https://review.monadnock.net.

23. "Mount Monadnock." Accessed February, 2023, https://altlasobscura.com.

24. Henry David Thoreau, referenced from his Journal in *Elevating Ourselves: Henry David Thoreau on Mountains*, sponsored by The Thoreau Society, ed. J. Parker, Huber, A Mariner Original, 1999, 63 and 71.

25. Ibid., 52-72.

Friendship - *Reciprocity*
The opening essay's context is taken from *A Week on the Concord and Merrimack Rivers* by Henry David Thoreau, Wednesday, 207-240.

26. Thoreau, *A Week*, 208.

27. Ibid., 217.

28. Ibid., 217.

29. Definition: https://oxfordlanguages.oup.com, Accessed January, 2023.

30. *Stone Age Economics*, 1972, identified by anthropologist Marshall Sahlins. Accessed January, 2023, https://files.libcom.org>files.

31. Henry David Thoreau, *A Week on the Concord and Merrimack Rivers*, Wednesday, 216.

32. Ibid., 216.

Tide of Circumstance – *Choice*
The opening essay's context is taken from *A Week on the Concord and Merrimack Rivers* by Henry David Thoreau, Wednesday, 234-237.

33. Thoreau, *A Week*, 236.

34. The Cornell Lab, Merlin app, "Herons, Ibis, and Allies, American Bittern." Accessed February, 2023.

35. Henry David Thoreau, *A Week on the Concord and Merrimack Rivers*, Wednesday, 190-191.

36. "Bittern Symbolism and Meaning," by Hailey Brophy, February 3, 2023. Accessed February, 2023, https://www.worldbirds.com.

*Walden*

The opening essay's context is taken from *Walden* by Henry David Thoreau, Historical Introduction by J. Lyndon Shanley, xvii-xxxv, Economy, 49.

Preserve Your True Course – *Authenticity*

The opening essay's context is taken from *Walden* by Henry David Thoreau, Economy, 70-72.

1. Thoreau, *Walden*, 71.
2. Ibid., 72.

Walden Pond – Day One

3. Henry David Thoreau, *Walden*, Visitors, 140.
4. Henry David Thoreau, *Walden*, The Pond in Winter, map of pond, 286.
5. Henry David Thoreau, *Walden*, Where I Lived, and What I Lived For, 90.

Where to Dwell? – *Passion*

The opening essay's context is taken from *Walden* by Henry David Thoreau, Solitude, 131-135.

6. Thoreau, *Walden*, 132.
7. Ibid., 133.
8. Henry David Thoreau, *The Journal 1837-1861*, ed. Damion Searls, October 22, 1837, age 36, 258-9.
9. Henry David Thoreau, *Walden*, Conclusion, 323.

Walden Pond – Day Two
Brister Freeman and Brister Hill's, *Humanities Magazine*, Feature article, "Black Walden" by Craig Lambert, September/October 2010, Volume 31, Number 5. Accessed January, 2023, https://www.neh.gov.

10. Henry David Thoreau, *Walking*, 5.

Earth's Eye – *Expression*
The opening essay's context is taken from *Walden* by Henry David Thoreau, Economy. 180-194.

11. Henry David Thoreau, *Walden*, The Ponds, 185.
12. Ibid., 175.
13. Ibid., 184.
14. Ibid., 185.
15. Ibid., 188.
16. Henry David Thoreau, *The Journal, 1837-1861,* ed. Damion Searls, December 2, 1840, age 23, 12.

The Life in Us – *Flow*
The opening essay's context is taken from *Walden* by Henry David Thoreau, Conclusion, 330-333.

17. Thoreau, *Walden*, 332.
18. Ibid., 333.
19. Ibid., 333.
20. "Panta Rhei: What Did Heraclitus Mean?" by Antonis Chaliakopouos, *MSc Museum Studies, BA History & Archaeology,* May 11, 2020. Accessed January, 2023, https://www.thecollector.com.
21. "Panta Rhei|Vocation, by iquillen, September 29, 2016. Accessed January, 2023, https://blogs.bu.edu.
22. Thoreau, *Walden*, Conclusion, 332.

Camp 19 – My Walden without the Pond
23. Henry David Thoreau, *Walden*, Solitude, 129.
24. Thoreau, *Walden*, Where I Lived and What I Lived For, 91.

25. Ibid., 82.

26. Henry David Thoreau, *The Journal, 1837-1861*, ed. Damion Searls, August 2, 1854, age 37, 272.

27. Thoreau, *Walden*, Where I Lived and What I Lived For, 89.

28. Thoreau, *Walden*, Sounds, 111.

29. Thoreau, *Walden*, Where I Lived and What I Lived For, 88.

30. Thoreau, *The Journal, 1837-1861*, ed. Damion Searls, August 2, 1854, age 37, 272.

## The Maine Woods

The opening essay's context is taken from *The Maine Woods* by Henry David Thoreau, Introduction by Edward Hoagland, ix-xxxiii.

1. Henry David Thoreau, *The Maine Woods*, Ktaadn 107.

Voyage of Discovery – *Recognition et al.*
The opening essay's context is taken from *The Maine Woods,* Ktaadn, 46-53.

2. Thoreau, *The Maine Woods*, 48.

3. Ibid., 50-51.

4. Ibid., 74.

Where Will You Go? – *Destination YOU!*
The opening essay's context is taken from *The Maine Woods,* Ktaadn, 98-103.

5. Henry David Thoreau, *The Journal, 1837-1861,* ed. Damion Searls, April 24, 1859, age 41, 563.

Summiting Mt. Megunticook, Camden Hills State Park
Context Information about Mount Megunticook referenced from "Mount Megunticook." https://www.summitpost.org, and the definition of Megunticook is referenced from Camden Hills

State Park. Accessed November, 2021, https://www.maine.gov>hikes.

6. Henry David Thoreau, *The Maine Woods*, Chesuncook, 114.

McGee Island, St. George, Maine
Information about McGee Island and the retreat center from The Salty Quill Writer's Retreat website, Accessed November, 2021, http://www.thesaltyquill.com.

7. Henry David Thoreau, *The Maine Woods*, Chesuncook, 114.

8. Zora Neale Hurston quote. Accessed January, 2023, https://www.zoranealehurston.com.

The Red Maple? - *Illusions*
The opening essay's context is taken from *The Maine Woods,* Chesuncook, 129-130.

9. Decoy definition from https://www.merriam-webster.com>decoy>definition and meaning. Accessed January, 2023.

10. Henry David Thoreau, *The Journal, 1837-1861,* ed. Damion Searls *61,* August 5, 1851, age 34, 65.

11. "What is self-awareness and why is it important?" Blog by Meredith Betz, September 14, 2022. Accessed January, 2023, https://www.betterup.com/blog/what-is-self-awareness.

12. Henry David Thoreau, *Letters to a Spiritual Seeker,* 38 and 60.

Spires – *Pillars of Life*
The opening essay's context is taken from *The Maine Woods,* Chesuncook, 151-165.

13. Thoreau, *Maine Woods*, 160-161.

14. Ibid., 163.

15. Ibid., 165.

16. Ibid., 166.

Summiting Mt. Kineo, Moosehead Lake
The opening essay's context and history from "Kineo, Mount." Accessed July, 2022, https://www.maineanencyclopedia.com.
17. Henry David Thoreau, *Walking*, 6.
18. Thoreau, *The Maine Woods*, The Allegash and East Branch, 239.
19. Ibid., 239-40.

Rogue Waves – *Expect the Unexpected*
The opening essay's context is taken from *The Maine Woods,* The Allegash and East Branch, 232-233. Moosehead Lake information taken from, "Moosehead Lake." Accessed January, 2023. https://wikipedia.org.
20. "Rogue Waves," Accessed, January, 2023. https://nationalgeographic.org.
21. Henry David Thoreau, *Walden.*

The Call of the Loon – Soul Sound
The opening essay's context is taken from *The Maine Woods,* The Allegash and East Branch, 303-308.
22. Henry David Thoreau quote, *The Journal, 1837-1861,* ed. Damion Searls, July 16, 1851, age 34, 60.
23. Thoreau, *The Journal,* March 10, 1841, age 23, cited there.
24. Henry David Thoreau's entire quote, "The mass of men lead lives of quiet desperation," *Walden,* Economy, 8.

Canoeing Prong Pond
Information about Prong Pond and map from *Quiet Water|Maine: AMC'S Canoe and Kayak*

*Guide to 157 of the Best Ponds, Lakes and Easy Rivers,* 3rd Edition, Alex Wilson and John Hayes.

25. Henry David Thoreau, *The Maine Woods*, Ktaadn, 88.
26. Henry David Thoreau, *Walking,* 30.

## Cape Cod

The opening essay's context is taken from *Cape Cod* by Henry David Thoreau, Introduction by Paul Theroux, vii-xvi.

1. Henry David Thoreau, *Cape Cod*, Provincetown, 319.

### Channeled Whelk – *Cycle of Life*

The opening essay's context is taken from *Cape Cod,* The Beach Again, 117-148.

2. "What is the Spiritual Meaning of a Spiral?" November 6, 2022. Accessed December, 2022, https://www.spiritualdesk.com.
3. Lyric, Accessed December, 2022. https://www.lyricfind.com.
4. Reference to Provincetown from *Cape Cod,* The Sea and The Desert, 229-230.
5. "How to Grow and Care for Balm of Gilead," by Erica Puisis, November 18, 2021. Accessed December, 2022, https://www.thespruce.com.
6. Henry David Thoreau, *The Journal, 1837-1861,* ed. Damion Searls, October 24, 1837, age 20, 3.

### Give Me Shelter – *Protection*

The opening essay's context and quotes taken from *Cape Cod,* The Beach, 63-74.

7. Henry David Thoreau, *Cape Cod,* The Beach, 74.
8. Ibid., 72.
9. "Genius Loci," Accessed January, 2023, https://en.m.wikipedia.org.

10. "Genius Loci-Designing Buildings." Accessed January, 2023, https://designingbuildings.co.uk.
11. "Education Resources and Facts," Accessed January, 2023, https://oceanservice.noaa.gov.
    Shipwrecked – *Preservation*
    The opening essay's context is taken from *Cape Cod,* Across the Cape, 160-162.
12. Thoreau, *Cape Cod*, 162.
13. *Ethical Wills: Putting Your Values on Paper* by Barry K. Baines, M.D., 2.

    Time and Tides – *Be Patient or Proceed?*
    The opening essay's context is taken from *Cape Cod,* Across the Cape, 163-173.
14. Thoreau, *Cape Cod*, 163.
15. Ibid., 173.
16. "Tides and Water Levels," by J.L. Sumich, 1996. Accessed January, 2023. https://www.oceanservice.noaa.gov.
17. "Do the Great Lakes have Tides:" by NOAA, January 20, 2023. Accessed January, 2023. https://www.oceanservice.noaa.gov.

    Seeds – *Lasting Blessings*
    The opening essay's context is taken from *Cape Cod,* The Highland Light, 192-194.
18. Thoreau, *Cape Cod.*, 194.
19. Ibid., 193.
20. Henry David Thoreau, *The Journal, 1837-1861,* ed. Damion Searls, September 28 1857, age 40, 456.
21. Henry David Thoreau, *Faith in a Seed: The Dispersion of Seeds & Other Late Natural History Writings,* opening quote.

Highland Light – A Beacon of Perspective
The opening essay's context is taken from *Cape Cod,* from his The Highland Light, 194-204. Information about the lighthouse from *Highland Light, This Little Booklet Tells You All About It* by Isaac Morton Small, Reprint Edition with Sequel – 2000.

22. *Highland Light, This Little Booklet Tells You All About It* by Isaac Morton Small, Reprint Edition with Sequel – 2000, 3.
23. Ibid., 3.
24. Henry David Thoreau, *Cape Cod,* The Highland Light, 202-203.
25. *Highland Light,* Isaac Morton Small, Reprint Edition with Sequel – 2000, Sequel, 1996.
26. Thoreau, *Cape Cod,* The Highland Light, 203-204.


*The Journal, 1837-1861*
1. Henry David Thoreau, *The Journal, 1837-1861,* ed. Damion Searls, October 22, 1837, age 20, 3.
2. Ibid., November 16, 1850, age 33, 44.


Dam It Up – *Don't Hold Back*
The opening essay's context is taken from *The Boatman: Henry David Thoreau's River Years* by Robert M. Thorson, 77. Thoreau's quote is indicated as an "omen of his future involvement in the flowage controversy" which would occur 21 years later.

3. Henry David Thoreau, *The Journal, 1837-1861,* ed. Damion Searls, February 12, 1851, age 33, 47.


Kayaking the Confluence
The opening essay's context is taken from "River Confluence Trail Guide," Division of Natural Resources, Concord, MA, 2015.

4. "River Confluence Trail Guide," Division of Natural Resources, Concord, MA, 2015.
5. Ibid.
6. "The Shot Heard Round the World: The Battles of Lexington and Concord," "Concord Hymn" by Ralph Waldo Emerson. Accessed February, 2023. https://constitutionfacts.com.

The Tight Ship – *Buoyancy*
The opening essay's context is taken from *The Boatman: Henry David Thoreau's River Years* by Robert M. Thorson, 75-76.

7. Definition: Accessed January, 2023. https://www.oxfordlanguages.com.
8. Definition: Accessed January, 2023. https://www.oxfordlanguages.com.
9. "Hull of a Ship-Understanding Design and Characteristics," by Soumya Chakraborty, February 19, 2021. Accessed January, 2023. https://marineinsight.com.
10. "What is the strongest and weakest part of a ship?" Accessed January, 2023. https://www.quora.com.

Mansion of the Air – *The Art of Listening*
The opening essay's context is taken from *The Journal, 1837-1861*, ed. Damion Searls, age 38, 376-378.

11. Searls, *The Journal*, April 9, 1856, age 38, 378.
12. Henry David Thoreau, *Walden,* Visitors, 140-141.
13. Henry David Thoreau, "Life Without Principle" as reprinted in *The Portable Thoreau,* 631.

I Walk Alone – *Solitude*
The opening essay's context is taken from *The Journal, 1837-1861*, ed. Damion Searls, age 37, 327-329.

14. Searls, *The Journal*, June 11, 1855, age 37, 327.

15. Ibid., June 11, 1855, age 37, 328.
16. Ibid., June 11, 1855, age 37, 328.
17. Ibid., referencing September 16, 1855, age 38, 328.
18. "Hummingbird Migration." Accessed January 15, 2023. https://hummingbirdcentral.com.
19. "Birds who fly Solo," by Jahangup. Accessed January 15, 2023, https://vocal.Media>beat.
20. "Eagles Fly Alone: Soar High and Make Your Own Path" by Livia, August 22, 2022. Accessed January 15, 2023, https://www.booksnbackpacks.com.

Summiting Mt. Wachusett, Massachusetts
The opening essay's context is taken from *Elevating Ourselves: Henry David Thoreau on Mountains,* ed. J. Parker Huber, A Mariner Original, 1999, 10-15 and Thoreau's essay, "A Walk to Wachusett," published in the Boston Miscellany of Literature, January 1843, 31-36.

21. Henry David Thoreau, *Walden*, Conclusion, 323.
22. Henry David Thoreau, "A Walk to Wachusett," published in the Boston Miscellany of Literature, January, 1843, 31-36.

Snow, the Great Revealer – *What is Visible? Or Not?*
The opening essay's context is taken from *The Journal, 1837-1861*, ed. Damion Searls, age 36, 240-244.

23. Searls, *The Journal*, January 1, 1854, age 36, 244.
24. "Science Time: Why does it get so quiet after it snows?" by Mary Mays and Nexstar Media Wire and contribution by The Associated Press. Accessed January 15, 2023, https://www.wric.com>weather.

Let's Go to the Moon! – *Reach and Soar*
The opening essay's context is taken from *The Journal, 1837-1861*, ed. Damion Searls, age 34, 74-78.

25. Searls, *The Journal,* September 4, 1851, age 34, 74.
26. Ibid., September 4, 1851, age 34, 75-77.
27. "NASA Artemis," NASA official Brian Dunbar. Accessed January, 2023, https://www.nasa.gov>Artemis.
28. Searls, *The Journal,* June 13, 1851, age 33, 55.
29. Henry David Thoreau. (n.d). AZQuotes.com. Accessed March 31, 2023, from AZQuotes.com, https://www.azquotes.com/quote/722205.

Summiting Mt. Katahdin, Baxter State Park, Maine
The context of this personal story comes from three sources: 1. *Elevating Ourselves: Henry David Thoreau on Mountains,* ed. J. Parker Huber, A Mariner Original, 1999, 27-35, 2. *The Maine Woods* by Henry David Thoreau, Ktaadn, 74-111, and 3. "Wildnotes," A Visitor's Guide to Baxter State Park," 2021.

1. Henry David Thoreau, *The Maine Woods*, Ktaadn, 84.
2. "Wildnotes," A Visitor's Guide to Baxter State Park," 2021.
3. Ibid.
4. Ibid.
5. Thoreau, *The Maine Woods,* Ktaadn, 75.
6. Ibid., 84.
7. Ibid., 80.
8. Ibid., 85.
9. Ibid., 84.

Reverence – *What is Sacred to You?*
The opening essay's context is taken from *The Journal, 1837-1861*, ed. Damion Searls, age 34, 73-78.

1. Searls, *The Journal*, September 3, 1851, age 34, 73.
2. Ibid., September 7, 1851, age 34, 76.
3. Ibid., September 7, 1851, age 34, 77.
4. Henry David Thoreau, *Letters to a Spiritual Seeker*, 158.
5. Searls, *The Journal*, May 6, 1854, age 36, 259.
6. Ibid., October 18, 1855, age 38, 333.

It Takes a Village – Thoreau College, Viroqua, Wisconsin
The context of this personal story comes from five sources: 1. *The Journal, 1837-1861,* ed. Damion Searls, age 43, 659-664, 2. "Every Root an Anchor: Wisconsin's Famous and Historic Trees," R. Bruce Allison, Madison, WI, Wisconsin Historical Society Press, 2005  3. Eagle Ridge Environmental Learning Center, Accessed January, 2023, https://www.eaglebluffmn.org, 4. Thoreau College Semester Programs [Brochure], 2022, and 5. Henry David Thoreau, *Walden*, Reading.

1. Henry David Thoreau, *Walden*, Reading, 109.
2. Ibid, 110.
3. "Every Root an Anchor: Wisconsin's Famous and Historic Trees," R. Bruce Allison, Madison, WI, Wisconsin Historical Society Press, 2005.
4. Eagle Ridge Environmental Learning Center, Accessed January, 2023, https://www.eaglebluffmn.org.
5. Thoreau College Semester Programs [Brochure], 2022.
6. Ibid.
7. Ibid.

Parting Thoughts

1. "Henry David Thoreau in Concord-Spiritual Travels," https://spiritualtravels.info/spiritual-sites-around-the-world/north-america/the-transcendentalist-trail-ion-concord-massachusetts/henry-david-thoreau-in-concord/. Accessed March 20, 2023.

2. "Henry David Thoreau-Wikipedia," Accessed March 20, 2023, https://en.m.wikipedia.org.

3. "Henry David Thoreau in Concord-Spiritual Travels," https://spiritualtravels.info/spiritual-sites-around-the-world/north-america/the-transcendentalist-trail-ion-concord-massachusetts/henry-david-thoreau-in-concord/. Accessed March 20, 2023.

4. "Ralph Waldo Emerson's Tribute to Henry David Thoreau-The Atlantic," https://www.theatlantic.com/magazine/archive/1862/08/thoreau/306418. Accessed March 20, 2023.

5. "President's Column: On Extinction and Magnificence" by Rochelle L. Johnson, "Thoreau Society Bulletin," ISSN 0040-6406, Number 320, Winter, 2023, 15.

6. "The Living Philosophy of Henry David Thoreau," https://www.thelivingphilosophy.com/henry-david-thoreau-living-philosophy/. Accessed April 9, 2023.

7. The Conversation, published October 26, 2022. https://theconversation.com/by-fact-checking-thoreaus-observations-at-walden-pond-we-showed-how-old-diaries-and-specimens-can-inform-modern-research-190304. Accessed April 9, 2023.

8. "A new program in Canada gives doctors the option of prescribing national park visits," published February 9, 2022, by Sharon Pruitt-Young. https://theconversation.com/by-fact-checking-thoreaus-observations-at-walden-

pond-we-showed-how-old-diaries-and-
specimens-can-inform-modern-research-
190304. Accessed April 9, 2023.

9.  Florence Williams, *The Nature Fix: Why Nature
    Makes Us Happier, Healthier, and More Creative*,
    19.

10. "Ecotherapy: Bringing nature into Treatment,"
    created April 1, 2020, Vol. 51, No. 3,
    https://www.apa.org/monitor/2020/04/natur
    e-sidebar. Accessed April 9, 2023.

11. Dr. Masaru Emoto, *The Healing Power of Water*,
    143-44.

12. Wallace J. Nichols, *Blue Mind*, back cover.

13. Henry David Thoreau, *Walden*, Spring, 317.

14. Florence Williams, *The Nature Fix: Why Nature
    Makes Us Happier, Healthier, and More Creative*,
    196.

15. Richard Louv, *The Nature Principle*, inside
    jacket cover.

16. Henry David Thoreau, *Walden*, Reading,
    107.

17. Ibid, 102.


Nature and Truth – *Thoreau's Spirituality*
The entire context and all quotes for this section
are taken from *The Journal, 1837-1861*, ed.
Damion Searls.

1.  Searls, *The Journal*, September 7, 1851, age 34,
    77.

# About the Author

Mary Anne Smrz is an avid kayaker who uses insights gained on the water to enrich her own life and the lives of others. She finds depth and meaning in her life from the solitude of kayaking and spending time in the restorative sanctuary of the natural world.

In her Reflections from the Red Kayak series, she offers insights on how lessons learned on the water help us all to navigate the uncharted waters of life.

A number of years ago, while caught in a cycle of grief, Mary Anne kayaked her way to healing. Because of the restorative benefits she experienced on the water, Mary Anne thought others could receive the same.

She founded and guided the Red Kayak Institute from 2012-2019, leading kayaking retreats for cancer survivors, caregivers, fundraising retreats for local scholarship funds, retreats for women in 12-step recovery programs, writer's workshops and more.

Today, Mary Anne offers her individual services as a kayaking retreat facilitator in collaboration with other nonprofit groups and organizations.

She writes from her home in Wisconsin.

Photo by Julie Christmas
Long Lake, Adirondack Mountains

313

Made in the USA
Monee, IL
01 March 2024

53883942R00184